SpringerBriefs in

For further volumes:
http://www.springer.com/series/8914

Poulomee Datta

Students with Intellectual Disabilities

Insights, Implications and Recommendations

Springer

Poulomee Datta
Faculty of Education
Australian Catholic University
Brisbane, QL
Australia

ISSN 2211-1921   ISSN 2211-193X (electronic)
ISBN 978-981-287-016-2   ISBN 978-981-287-017-9 (eBook)
DOI 10.1007/978-981-287-017-9
Springer Singapore Heidelberg New York Dordrecht London

Library of Congress Control Number: 2014934459

Printed on acid-free paper

Springer is part of Springer Science+Business Media (www.springer.com)

Preface

There is an absence of research in Australia on self-concept in students with disabilities although such testing is taken for granted among students without disabilities. This study investigated the self-concept of the students with intellectual disabilities who were placed in specialist and mainstream educational settings in South Australia. The qualitative study aimed to gain insights into what students with intellectual disabilities felt about themselves and their achievements across the different dimensions of self-concept.

This research was divided into two stages of execution. In Stage 1, the Tennessee Self-Concept questionnaire was administered to 20 students with intellectual disabilities. In Stage 2, interviews were conducted with nine students with intellectual disabilities, as well as a total of five parents and four teachers. These data reflected a range of viewpoints from which to examine the research questions.

Although the majority of the students with intellectual disabilities obtained low scores on all dimensions of self-concept- physical, moral, personal, family, social and academic, some students obtained normal scores in relation to family and academic self-concepts. Some of the factors responsible for the low self-concept scores were identified through the interviews. Notable among them were lack of independence, students' cognitive deficits, depression and mood swings commonly experienced by these students, degree and severity of impairment (the greater the impairment the lower the self-concept), negative behavior demonstrated by non-disabled peers, bullying, lack of support from mainstream peers, inexperienced and unskilled teachers, inadequate family support, step-parent households, lack of confidence, exclusion in mainstream classes, students with intellectual disabilities experienced failure too often and too early and these students took more time and required extra effort to learn and grasp new concepts. These findings have implications for teachers, special educators, policy makers, and a range of professionals in the education and special education sector in enabling greater understanding of the problems experienced by these students and pointing to modifications and improvements in the services for these students.

Acknowledgments

My sincere thanks go to my three mentors, Prof. Tania Aspland, Associate Professor Carolyn Palmer, and Dr. Margaret Secombe. Their rigor, scholarship, and professional guidance, delivered with such grace and good humour, have challenged and invigorated my learning.

I am indebted to the several school and college Principals who agreed to allow me to collect my data from their school/institutes. I would like to acknowledge the assistance given by teachers who assisted in recruiting participants, providing information, and participating in the research interviews. Their professionalism, warmth, and enthusiasm were most important during the data collection phase. My thanks go also to the students and parents who so willingly participated in the study.

My thanks also go to my family for their patience, tolerance, undying support, and encouragement. I pay tribute to my parents, Pulak and Mita Datta, who instilled in me the values of pride, hard work, and learning. Their love, support, and understanding has been one of the main driving forces behind my academic pursuits. Finally, this book would never have been completed without the consistent assistance and encouragement offered by my husband, Joy Talukdar, who has always been a source of inspiration for my work. Joy, your considerable forbearance, and personal support enabled me to write this book. This book is dedicated to you!

Contents

Chapter 1
Self-Concepts of Students with Intellectual Disabilities

Abstract Positive self-concept is a variable which influences considerably on the well-being and total development of students in general. Thus, this aspect is of particular importance in the special education context as well. This chapter outlines the rationale and purpose of investigating self-concept in students with intellectual disabilities. It also traces the development of students with disabilities in the history of special education in Australia. An overview of the South Australian context is also provided. The aims and research questions designed for this study in relation to students with intellectual disabilities are provided. The limitations and delimitations of this study along with the definition of some key terms are further discussed.

Keywords Self-concept · Students with disabilities · Students with intellectual disabilities · Specialist and mainstream settings · South Australia

1.1 Introduction

Intellectual disability can impact on students' learning with the result they may experience difficulties in school and home (Fitts 1996). Some of these students may develop poor self-concept (Lucy 1997). This study investigates the self-concept of students with intellectual disabilities in South Australia. The focus is on self-concept across six dimensions namely: Physical, Moral, Personal, Family, Social and Academic Self-Concepts and Total Self-Concept. This study further provides insights into what students with intellectual disabilities are able to achieve in the different dimensions of self-concept and highlights the reasons for high or low self-concept in these students. Self-concept is used as the key variable to unveil some of the social, personal, family and academic problems faced by these students.

There is some variability in the distribution of disability reported across States and Territories in Australia. The disability prevalence rate is highest in Tasmania followed by South Australia and lowest in the Northern Territory and Australian

P. Datta, *Students with Intellectual Disabilities*, SpringerBriefs in Education,
DOI: 10.1007/978-981-287-017-9_1, © The Author(s) 2014

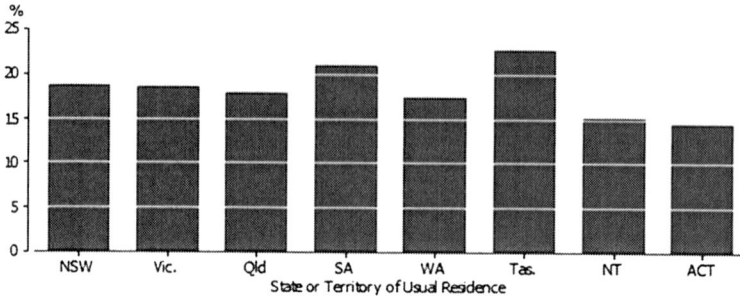

Fig. 1.1 ABS survey of disability (Ageing and Carers 2009 cited in ABS 2011)

Capital Territory. Figure 1.1, presents the prevalence of disabilities across States and Territories in Australia.

South Australia is the chosen context for this study because it is the State with the second highest prevalence of disabilities in Australia. Intellectual disability is a major disability in the Australian population, especially among children and young adults (Australian Institute of Health and Welfare [AIHW] 2008). Over half a million Australians have intellectual disabilities (AIHW 2008). People with intellectual disabilities are a major group of users of disability support services in Australia (AIHW 2005, 2007), which could stand alone be an imperative rationale to study this cohort. The estimated number of people with intellectual disabilities in South Australia in 2003 was 52,600 (AIHW 2008). Intellectual impairments are often diagnosed early in a person's life and generally affect the younger population (42 % were aged less than 25 compared with 26 % aged 65 years or more) (Commonwealth of Australia 2000). Thus, the age range of the students with intellectual disabilities in this study ranged from 15 to 25 years.

Research worldwide has substantiated that disabilities, in general can impact negatively on the self-concept of a student (Elbaum and Sharon 2001; Hancock 2001; Heiman and Precel 2003; Peleg 2009; Sharma et al. 2004). Despite having these data on the prevalence of intellectual disabilities in Australia, little information is available on the impact that intellectual loss can have on these students' self-concepts, making it a critical area of investigation.

1.2 Background to the Study

The following subsections trace the historical development of students with disabilities in Australia over a specific period of time. Further, the South Australian background for this study is provided.

1.2.1 Historical Perspective in Australia

Between the 1940s and the 1970s school systems in Australia began to establish a large number of segregated special schools to cater for students with specific disabilities. Public school systems were provided only for students who were deemed to be 'educable' or 'trainable' and during this time many children with profound support needs were not offered places even in special schools (Loreman et al. 2005 as cited in Forlin 2006, p. 266). In the early 1970s, the Karmel Report (Karmel 1973), Schools in Australia, recommended Government support for integration, resulting in Commonwealth funding being directed to Government schools in 1974 and extended to the private sectors in 1975. In the 1970s whilst acknowledging the recommendations of the Karmel Report and international declarations that were enacted on the rights of the child, discussions commenced about increasing regular class placements for children with disabilities (Forlin 2006, p. 266).

It was not until 1981 (International Year of Disabled Persons) that the first major attempt to promote greater acceptance and integration of people with disabilities occurred on a large scale in Australia (Carroll et al. 2003 as cited in Forlin 2006, p. 266). At the same time in the United States, professional advocacy groups claimed that the legislation did not go far enough. They therefore, launched the Regular Education Initiative (REI) movement, which called for the merging of special and general education into one single system in which all children attended the regular community school. The REI maintained that all special education staff, resources and learners with special needs should be integrated into the regular school (Kisanji 1999). Countries such as Australia and New Zealand left the debate open, but emphasised parental choice (Kisanji 1999). By the end of 1981 every jurisdiction in Australia had a policy on students with disabilities and the idea of integration was emerging slowly and beginning to become a reality in schools (Carroll et al. 2003 as cited in Forlin 2006, p. 266). During the past two decades, there has been a slow but consistent movement across all states and territories in Australia towards the inclusion of children with mild to severe disabilities in regular classrooms (Ashman and Elkins 1997; Forlin 1998). Since then there has been a parallel and increasing momentum towards integrating people with disabilities into the mainstream of all aspects of society. However, there have been cases which have challenged regular class placements for children with disabilities in Australia (Forlin and Forlin 1998). When students are placed in positive environments such as general classrooms it can be a place for growth, development and well-being (Sale and Carey 1995). Students with disabilities have equal rights to access free education in the least restrictive environment and with adequate supports, as has been legislated in countries like the US (Forlin and Forlin 1998; Pivik et al. 2002). In Australia and New Zealand, it remains a matter of policy, not law.

The Salamanca Statement in 1994 states that those who have special educational needs must have access to regular schools which should accommodate them within a child-centred pedagogy capable of meeting these needs. However, schools in Australia in the 1990s have predominantly been exclusive institutions and have failed to attain inclusion status (Slee 1996). Forlin and Forlin (1998) further argued that despite the complex arrangement of laws and policies for education in Australia, there is no legal mandate to ensure inclusive education.

The integration of students with disabilities required children to be registered in a separate facility or class within a regular school, and then provided with opportunities to participate in the mainstream setting (Forlin 2006). In Australia, this meant that students with disabilities (which included students with intellectual disabilities) were increasingly registered in their local regular school. They may be withdrawn for parts of the school day to receive intensive intervention programs by a specialist support teacher (Forlin 2006). This option was prevalent in the early 2000s and was usually determined by the school considering whether it was able to provide for a student before offering them a mainstream placement (Forlin 2006). Following the publication of the Salamanca Statement (UNESCO 1994) the focus of education has gradually moved towards the inclusive movement (Forlin 2006). Inclusion, however, remains a challenging prospect in secondary schools. Forlin (2006) further indicated that after the implementation of the Salamanca Statement, inclusivity has been an evolving paradigm in Australia yet some schools are failing to attain it as they are led by unresponsive bureaucracies, teacher unions more concerned with ideology than supporting what happens in the classroom (Donnelly 2004, p. 2). Inclusion is used here to represent the education of all students in general classrooms.

Tenets of the inclusion concept, according to Elkins (2009, p. 41) are as follows: complete acceptance of a student with a disability or other marginalised students in a regular class, with appropriate changes being made to ensure that the student is fully involved in all class activities. Thus, inclusion is characterised by the redesign of regular schools both physically and in curriculum, to provide for the complete education of all students who seek to attend (Ashman and Elkins 2009). Pearce and Forlin (2005) indicated that many of the changes occurring in education systems within Australia were conducive to inclusion. The movement towards the inclusion of students with disabilities occurred in 2006 in most states in Australia, with the degree and outcome being quite varied as it continues to rely upon independent arrangements at each school site (Forlin 2006). As a consequence today, the majority of students with disabilities attend general education classrooms alongside peers who are non-disabled in Australia and in most parts of the developed world. Along with Special Education centres highly specialized inclusive schools have also been developed (Early Childhood Resource Teachers Network Ontario 1997; Irwin et al. 2000). Both of these types of educational settings provide a variety of support mechanisms to develop the students academically and socially.

Carrington and Robinson (2004) indicated that the Index for Inclusion (Booth et al. 2000) provided a useful framework for professional development related to inclusive schooling in Queensland, Australia. The Index for Inclusion is a unique set of materials designed to support schools in a process of inclusive school development. The Index is concerned with improving school attainments through inclusive practices and it does this for all pupils. The Index for Inclusion was developed in the UK at the Centre for Studies in Inclusive Education (CSIE) by Tony Booth and Mel Ainscow. In March 2000, these resources were released by the Department of Education to all government schools in the UK (Carrington and Elkins 2002; Vaughan 2002).

Recent research on inclusion in Australia (Anderson et al. 2007; Forlin 2006; Subban and Sharma 2006;) suggests that though some schools, teachers and parents have been very positive towards inclusion, a number of obstacles and barriers have arisen in implementing it in the regular classrooms. Over the past five years, all Australian states and territories, education departments and non-government sectors have continued to evolve and reconstruct themselves and inclusive education has been high on the agenda (Ashman and Elkins 2009). Despite the widespread appeal of inclusion as a social justice ideal, the educational outcomes and general wellbeing of students with special educational needs and disabilities has not been fully explored (Ashman and Elkins 2009). Since research has identified self-concept as one of the key variables among others in improving the general wellbeing and educational outcomes for students (Fitts and Warren 2003; Halder and Datta 2012), this facet have been chosen to investigate in students with intellectual disabilities in South Australia.

1.2.2 The South Australian Context of the Study

The Department for Education and Child Development (DECD) is responsible for ensuring the provision of children's services and public education throughout South Australia. The DECD provides the Disabilities Support Programme wherein additional support is provided to support learners with disabilities to work alongside learners without disabilities, in mainstream settings (Department for Education and Child Development [DECD] 2012). The DECD provides a range of learning and teaching materials, resources and specialized services which support children and students with disabilities in mainstream and specialist schools in South Australia (DECD 2012). Despite the provision of these support services, research on the self-concept of students with disabilities is still in its embryonic stage.

1.3 Statement of the Problem

Self-concept is an issue which impacts significantly on the well-being and total personality development of students in general (Broderick and Blewitt 2006; Hadley et al. 2008). Thus, this aspect is of particular importance in the special education context. Research has identified self-concept as a desirable goal for all students (Palmer 2003; Halder and Datta 2012); however, it is of particular importance for students who may be perceived as vulnerable such as those with disabilities (Craven et al. 2003; Zetlin and Turner 1988). An adolescent's self-concept is dynamic, intricate and irregularly patterned (Inhelder and Piaget 1958). That is difficulties and conflicts in the adolescent and young adulthood stages can lower self-concept which can result problems in academic, behaviour, adjustment to peers and family relationships. Adolescents with intellectual disabilities are further prone to feelings of inadequacy and inferiority (Beaty 1991) which casts a negative influence on their self-concept, making it a critical area of study. When the Australian government has placed students with special educational needs and inclusivity in mainstream classrooms as one of its top priorities (Aspland and Datta 2011), it is surprising that most of the self-concept research has been directed towards students without disabilities, and students with disabilities have been excluded from the realm of self-concept research. While research has identified that self-concept is a key factor in students' school success (Kanu 2002; Swanson 2003), it is appalling that in the era of equality, mainstreaming and inclusion, there is no research to date to investigate the different dimensions of self-concept among students with intellectual disabilities and the factors associated with it, particularly in South Australia.

1.4 Purpose of the Research

The purpose of this study is to investigate the self-concepts of the students with intellectual disabilities who are placed in specialist and mainstream settings in South Australia. This study also aims to determine what are students with intellectual disabilities able to achieve in the different dimensions of self-concept and provide insights into the reasons for high or low self concept of the students under consideration. The students with intellectual disabilities include adolescents in high schools and adults placed in Technical and Further Education (TAFE) Institutes.

1.5 Aims of the Research

This study, designed to investigate the self-concepts among students with intellectual disabilities, has two broad aims. The first aim is to explore the nature of self-concept across the dimensions namely: Physical, Moral, Personal, Family, Social, Academic and thus, total self-concept of a group of female and male students with intellectual disabilities.

The second aim is to provide insights into what students with intellectual disabilities are able to achieve in the different dimensions of self-concept and to investigate the reasons for low or high self-concept in the Physical, Moral, Personal, Family, Social and Academic areas.

1.6 Research Questions

The main research questions that emerge from the purpose and aims of the study in relation to students with intellectual disabilities are as follows:

- What are the scores of self-concept and its dimensions for the female and male students with intellectual disabilities in South Australia?
- What are students with intellectual disabilities able to achieve in the different dimensions of self-concept and why?

1.7 Significance of the Research

Research on self-concept worldwide has focused on the topic from psychological, educational and sociological perspectives. It is clear that this topic is important in a variety of fields and thus of value to study in the South Australian context.

Self-concept, which is considered to be an important facet for a child's social, psychological and educational development (Broderick and Blewitt 2006) has important implications for positive existence, and is a significant variable for achievement and optimistic development in the society in every sphere irrespective of whether they are disabled or not (Datta and Halder 2012). Students with disabilities are less likely to develop a positive self-concept compared to students without disabilities (Elbaum and Sharon 2001). Research has substantiated that the physical, personal, moral, social, family, intellectual and school status and academic dimensions of self-concept (which this study explores) are the key factors to establish the total and all round development of an individual and bring success for the individual in all future endeavours (Fitts and Warren 2003) in any educational context which schools need to bolster accordingly. In Australia, the importance of self-concept is highlighted in virtually all statements of the goals of education, and is seen as a means of facilitating desirable outcomes for all students (Purdie and McCrindle 2004). In spite of such explicit and overt declarations of the importance of self-concept, research in this arena is limited on students with disabilities.

Self-concept becomes more abstract and differentiated during adolescence and adulthood (Inhelder and Piaget 1958). Harter (1990) suggests that adolescents and young adults are often disturbed by conflicting views of self. Broderick and Blewitt (2006) have described these two stages as complex and multifaceted wherein physical and psychological changes commence. Adolescence and adulthood are the two most important stages of life and as children move further into their teenage years and connect to the adult world, they face unfamiliar territory. If any kind of impairment or disability is added to these difficult stages of life, it may become very complicated and convoluted for these students and they need all the help and support that can be provided. Thus, the reason for choosing the focus on adolescence and adulthood. It is clear that the development of self-concept cannot be left to chance for students with intellectual disabilities. Self-concept is an important goal for all students with disabilities (Palmer 2003). Programs need to be developed that address the systemic intervention and training of appropriate skills to develop the self-concept of students with disabilities (Palmer 2003), but before this training can occur, the level and nature of self-concept acquired by these students must be explored.

This research is significant in its aim to shed light on the physical, moral, personal, family, social, academic and total self-concepts of the students with intellectual disabilities and the reasons for their low or high self-concept in each of the dimensions as well as insights into how their experiences in their physical, moral, personal, family, social and academic lives impact outcomes on each of these dimensions. It will also contribute to the body of knowledge on the areas that serve as a catalyst to increase these problems for this group of students. In order to design effective programs to develop the self-concept of students with intellectual disabilities, teachers need to be aware of the factors that affect the different dimensions of self-concept of this group of students. This knowledge will place them in a better position to provide opportunities and implement strategies that increase the positive self-concept in such students.

It is anticipated that this research will be useful to students, teachers, parents, educational administrators and planners, counsellors and special educators who will be undertaking work in the field of Special Education particularly dealing with students having intellectual disabilities. The study is designed to add to current information in terms of program planning, and the provision of a safe, secure, positive learning environment for all students.

1.8 Limitations and Delimitations

1.8.1 Limitations of the Study

- The study was limited by the size of the sample that was selected for this study which was restricted by access to an already small population. Data were collected from multiple sources (students with intellectual disabilities, their parents and teachers). Although the number of participants in the groups investigated was low, the data collection was in depth.
- The data were collected in a State in Australia, which provided few subjects. The sensitivity of the area and the unwillingness of some parents to participate in the study, further limited access to subjects. Because of the low numbers of students with intellectual disabilities available for the study, findings must be interpreted with care.

1.8.2 Delimitations of the Study

- The study was limited to an investigation of only one group of students: those with intellectual disabilities.
- The sample undertaken for this study was limited to adolescents attending state specialist and regular schools in South Australia (it did not include adolescent students attending schools in the Catholic and Independent sectors) and adults attending South Australian TAFE Institutes (it did not include adult students attending Universities).
- In this study, only students with mild intellectual disabilities were included as students with moderate, severe and profound intellectual disabilities would not be able to comprehend the questionnaires properly.

1.9 Definition of Terms

1.9.1 Intellectual Disability

The American Association on Intellectual and Developmental Disabilities (AAIDD) defines Intellectual Disability as a "disability characterized by significant limitations both in intellectual functioning and in adaptive behaviour as expressed in conceptual, social and practical adaptive skills" (Hallahan et al. 2009, p. 147). This research only included students with diagnosed mild intellectual disabilities.

1.9.2 Self-Concept

Self-Concept refers to the complex system of learned beliefs, opinions and attitudes a person has about himself or herself (Palmer 2003).

1.10 Book Structure

This book has been organised into eight chapters. Chapter 1 introduces the study, outlines the purpose and significance of the research, states the aims and the research questions, defines key terms and explains the study's limitations and delimitations.

Chapter 2 analyses and synthesises the views of researchers in the field on self-concept for students with disabilities with a particular focus on intellectual disability. Collectively the previous studies discussed sketch a holistic picture of the current state of self-concept for students with intellectual disabilities and establish the context for this research.

Chapter 3 provides the theoretical framework for the research. The Shavelson et al. (1976) and Marsh and Shavelson (1985) models of self-concept and other recent research studies (Duvdevany 2002; Tracey and Marsh 2002) formed the basis for the different dimensions of self-concept used in this study.

Chapter 4 outlines the research methodology and design. In this chapter, the research paradigm is identified, the research questions restated, and an overview of the research design provided. The research methods are explicated and the strategies for data collection and analysis are detailed, along with ethical considerations.

Chapter 5 reports and analyses the Stage 1 survey questionnaire data around themes namely: Physical, Moral, Personal, Family, Social, Academic and Total self-concepts. To present the questionnaire data, descriptive statistics is used in the form of percentages in each theme to identify the incidence of high, average or low cases across gender in students with intellectual disabilities.

Chapter 6 reports and analyses the Stage 2 interview responses around themes namely: Physical, Moral, Personal, Family, Social and Academic self-concepts. The data from interviews with students with intellectual disabilities, their parents and teachers are presented under each theme.

Chapter 7 discusses and interprets the collective findings (questionnaire and interview data) from Chaps. 5 and 6 on self-concept. In this Chapter, the findings are supported and contrasted by the literature, wherever possible.

Finally, Chapter 8 presents the structure of the entire study, together with the research questions and answers provided to each research question are restated. The implications for educational policy and practice and future research with reference to the research findings, and the conclusions are also provided.

References

Anderson, C. J. K., Klassen, R. M., & Georgiou, G. K. (2007). Inclusion in Australia: What teachers say they need and what school psychologists can offer. *School Psychology International, 28*(2), 131–147. doi:10.1177/0143034307078086.

Ashman, A. F., & Elkins, J. (1997). *Educating children with special needs.* Sydney: Prentice Hall.

Ashman, A. F., & Elkins, J. (Eds.). (2009). *Educating for inclusion and diversity* (3rd ed.). Frenches Forest: NSW Pearson Education Australia.

Aspland, T., & Datta, P. (2011). Insights into the school reporting policies across Australia for students with special needs. *Curriculum and Teaching, 26*(2), 73–83.

Australian Bureau of Statistics. (2011). *Disability prevalence* (Report No. 4446.0–Disability, Australia, 2009). Canberra: ABS. Retrieved from http://www.abs.gov.au/ausstats/abs@.nsf/Lookup/4446.0main+features42009

Australian Institute of Health and Welfare. (2005). *Australia's welfare 2005.* (Cat. no. AUS 65). Canberra: AIHW.

Australian Institute of Health and Welfare. (2007). *Disability support services 2005–2006: National data on services provided under the Commonwealth state/Territory disability agreement.* (Cat. no. DIS 51. Disability Series). Canberra: AIHW.

Australian Institute of Health and Welfare. (2008). *Disability in Australia: Intellectual disability*. Bulletin no. 67. Cat. no. AUS 110. Canberra: AIHW.

Beaty, L. A. (1991). The effects of visual impairment on adolescents' self-concept. *Journal of Visual Impairment and Blindness, 85*(3), 129–130.

Booth, T., Ainscow, M., Black-Hawkins, K., Vaughan, M., & Shaw, L. (2000). *Index for inclusion: Developing learning and participation in schools*. Bristol: Centre for Studies on Inclusive Education (CSIE).

Broderick, P. C., & Blewitt, P. (2006). *The life span: Human development for helping professionals* (2nd ed.). Upper Saddle River, NJ: Pearson, Education Inc.

Carrington, S., & Elkins, J. (2002). Comparison of a traditional and an inclusive secondary school culture. *International Journal of Inclusive Education, 6*(1), 1–16. doi:10.1080/13603110110061754.

Carrington, S., & Robinson, R. (2004). A case study of inclusive school development: A journey of learning. *International Journal of Inclusive Education, 8*(2), 141–153. doi:10.1080/1360311032000158024.

Commonwealth of Australia. (2000). *1998 disability, ageing and carers: Disability and long term health conditions (Report No. 4433.0)*. Retrieved from http://www.abs.gov.au/AUSSTATS/abs@.nsf/Lookup/4433.0Main+Features11998?OpenDocument

Craven, R. G., Marsh, H. W., & Burnett, P. (2003). Cracking the self-concept enhancement conundrum: A call and blueprint for the next generation of self-concept enhancement research. In H. W. Marsh, R. G. Craven, & D. McInerney (Eds.), *International advances in self research* (Vol. 1, pp. 91–126). Greenwich, CT: Information Age Publishing Inc.

Datta, P., & Halder, S. (2012). Insights into self-concept of the adolescents who are visually impaired in India. *International Journal of Special Education, 27*(2), 86–93.

Department for Education and Child Development. (2012). On the same basis: Implementing the disability discrimination act standards for Education. Adelaide: Government of South Australia. Retrieved from http://www.decd.sa.gov.au/speced/pages/specialneeds/OnthebamebasisDDAEducationStandards/?reFlag=1

Duvdevany, I. (2002). Self-concept and adaptive behaviour of people with intellectual disability in integrated and segregated recreation activities. *Journal of Intellectual Disability Research, 46*(5), 419–429. doi:10.1046/j.1365-2788.2002.00415.x.

Donnelly, K. (2004). *Why our schools are failing*. Sydney: Duffy and Snellgrove.

Early Childhood Resource Teachers Network Ontario. (1997). *Checklist for quality inclusive education: A self-assessment tool and manual for early childhood settings*. Barrie, ON: Author.

Elbaum, B., & Sharon, V. (2001). School-based interventions to enhance the self-concept of students with learning disabilities: A meta-analysis. *The Elementary School Journal, 101*(3), 303–329. doi:10.2307/1002249.

Elkins, J. (2009). Legislation, policies, and principles. In A. F. Ashman & J. Elkins (Eds.), *Education for inclusion and diversity* (3rd ed., pp. 35–56). Frenches Forest: NSW Pearson Education Australia.

Fitts, W. H. (1996). *Tennessee self-concept scale: Second edition manual*. Los Angeles, CA: Western Psychological Services.

Fitts, W. H., & Warren, W. L. (2003). *Tennessee self-concept scale manual* (2nd ed.). Los Angeles, CA: Western Psychological Services.

Forlin, C. (1998). Teachers' personal concerns about including children with a disability in regular classrooms. *Journal of Developmental and Physical Disabilities, 10*(1), 87–106. doi:10.1023/a:1022865618600.

Forlin, C. (2006). Inclusive education in Australia ten years after Salamanca. *European Journal of Psychology of Education—EJPE (Instituto Superior de Psicologia Aplicada), 21*(3), 265–277. doi:10.1007/BF03173415.

Forlin, P., & Forlin, C. (1998). Constitutional and legislative framework for inclusive education in Australia. *Australian Journal of Education, 42*(2), 204–217.

Hadley, A. M., Hair, E. C., & Moore, K. A. (2008). Assessing what kids think about themselves: A guide to adolescent self-concept for out-of-school time program practitioners. *Research-to-Results: Child Trends, 32.* Retrieved from http://childtrends.org/wp-content/uploads/2008/09/2008-32Self-Concept.pdf

Halder, S., & Datta, P. (2012). An exploration into self concept: A comparative analysis between the adolescents who are sighted and blind in India. *British Journal of Visual Impairment, 30*(1), 31–41. doi:10.1177/0264619611428202.

Hallahan, D. P., Kauffman, J. M., & Pullen, P. C. (2009). *Exceptional learners: An introduction to special education.* Boston: Allyn & Bacon.

Hancock, D. R. (2001). Effects of test anxiety and evaluative threat on students' achievement and motivation. *The Journal of Educational Research, 94*(5), 284–290. doi:10.1080/00220670109598764.

Harter, S. (1990). Issues in the assessment of the self-concept of children and adolescents. In A. M. L. Greca (Ed.), *Through the eyes of the child: Obtaining self-reports from children and adolescents* (pp. 292–325). Boston, MA: Allyn and Bacon.

Heiman, T., & Precel, K. (2003). Students with learning disabilities in higher education: Academic strategies profile. *Journal of Learning Disabilities, 36*(3), 248–258. doi:10.1177/002221940303600304.

Inhelder, B., & Piaget, J. (1958). *The growth of logical thinking from childhood to adolescence: An essay on the construction of formal operational structures.* New York: Basic Books.

Irwin, S. H., Lero, D. S., & Brophy, K. (2000). *A matter of urgency: Including children with special needs in child care in Canada.* Wreck Cove, NS: Breton Books.

Kanu, Y. (2002). In their own voices: first nations students identify some cultural mediators of their learning in the formal school system. *Alberta Journal of Educational Research, 48*(2), 98–121.

Karmel, P. (1973). *Schools in Australia: Report of the Interim Committee for the Australian Schools Commission* (0642949042). Canberra: Commonwealth of Australia.

Kisanji, J. (1999). *Historical and theoretical basis of inclusive education.* Paper presented at the Keynote address for the Workshop on Inclusive Education in Namibia: The Challenge for Teacher Education, Khomasdal, Windhoek, Namibia.

Lucy, Y. S. W. (1997). *Self-concept of visually impaired students in a mainstream secondary school in Hong Kong* (Master's thesis, The University of Hong Kong [Pokfulam, Hong Kong], Hong Kong). Retrieved from http://hub.hku.hk/handle/10722/28678

Marsh, H. W., & Shavelson, R. (1985). Self-concept: Its multifaceted, hierarchical structure. *Educational Psychologist, 20*(3), 107–123. doi:10.1207/s15326985ep2003_1.

Palmer, C. D. (2003). *Social competence of children with albinism.* Unpublished Ph.D. thesis, The University of Queensland, Queensland.

Pearce, M., & Forlin, C. (2005). Challenges and potential solutions for enabling inclusion in secondary schools. *Australasian Journal of Special Education, 29*, 93–105.

Peleg, O. (2009). Test anxiety, academic achievement, and self-esteem among Arab adolescents with and without learning disabilities. *Learning Disability Quarterly, 32*(1), 11–20.

Pivik, J., McComas, J., & Laflamme, M. (2002). Barriers and facilitators to inclusive education. *Exceptional Children, 69*(1), 97–107.

Purdie, N., & McCrindle, A. (2004). Measurement of self-concept among indigenous and non-indigenous Australian students. *Australian Journal of Psychology, 56*(1), 50–62. doi:10.1080/00049530410001688128.

Sale, P., & Carey, M. D. (1995). The sociometric status of students with disabilities in a full-inclusion school. *Exceptional Children, 62*, 6–19.

Sharma, N., Vaid, S., & Jamwal, Z. (2004). The concept of self in physically challenged institutionalized children. *Disability India Journal.*

Shavelson, R. J., Hubner, J. J., & Stanton, G. C. (1976). Self-concept: Validation of construct interpretations. *Review of Educational Research, 46*(3), 407–441.

Slee, R. (1996). Inclusive schooling in Australia? Not yet! *Cambridge Journal of Education, 26*(1), 19–33. doi:10.1080/0305764960260102.

Subban, P., & Sharma, U. (2006). Teachers' perceptions of inclusive education in Victoria. *Australia. International Journal of Special Education, 21*(1), 42–52.

Swanson, S. (2003). Motivating learners in northern communities. *Canadian Journal of Native Education, 27*(1), 61–73.

Tracey, D. K., & Marsh, H. W. (2002). Self-concepts of preadolescents with mild intellectual disability: Multidimensionality, measurement, and support for the big fish little pond effect. *Self-Concept Research: Driving International Research Agendas, 35*, 419–427.

UNESCO. (1994). *The Salamanca statement and framework for action on special needs education*. Paris: UNESCO.

Vaughan, M. (2002). An index for inclusion. *European Journal of Special Needs Education, 17*(2), 197–201. doi:10.1080/08856250210139316.

Zetlin, A. G., & Turner, J. L. (1988). Salient domains in the self-conception of adults with mental retardation. *Mental Retardation, 26*(4), 219–222.

Chapter 2
Literature Review

Abstract This chapter discusses a whole landscape of relevant issues related to the self-concept of individuals with disabilities, in particular children, adolescents and adults with intellectual disabilities. The self-concept literature amongst this cohort is traced and thoroughly critiqued and some limitations identified through this progression are presented. The impact of school placement and stigma on self-concept is further reviewed. Collectively the research studies sketch a holistic picture of the current state of research on self-concept for students with intellectual disabilities.

Keywords Self-concept and intellectual disabilities · Children with intellectual disabilities · Adolescents with intellectual disabilities · Adults with intellectual disabilities · Stigma and self-concept

2.1 Introduction

This chapter presents an extensive review of the empirical research that shapes the argument for the significance of the research. A range of carefully selected scholarly works were surveyed in order to refine understanding of topics relevant to this study. This chapter is organised under one main section: 'why study self-concept'. Exploration of this topic in international and Australian research identified gaps in the literature related to the research questions indicated in Chap. 1. This section provides an overview of the relationship between self-concept and disabilities. This section also analyses the research on self-concept and intellectual disabilities, with particular emphasis on children, adolescents and adults with intellectual disabilities. In addition, research studies on the impact of school placement and stigma on self-concept are considered under this section.

P. Datta, *Students with Intellectual Disabilities*, SpringerBriefs in Education, DOI: 10.1007/978-981-287-017-9_2, © The Author(s) 2014

2.2 Why Study Self-Concept?

Self-concept is generally considered to be "the totality of a complex, organized, and dynamic system of learned beliefs, attitudes and opinions that each person holds to be true about his or her personal existence" (Purkey 1988, p. 2). Franken (1994, p. 443) states that "there is a great deal of research which shows that the self-concept is, perhaps, the basis for all motivated behaviour". He argues that "it is the self-concept that gives rise to possible selves, and it is possible selves that create the motivation for behaviour" (Franken 1994, p. 443).

Self-concept is a significant and exhaustive area which forms an important part of one's personality. According to Snygg and Combs (1949), self-concept, something beneath one's skin, which affects one's behaviour, is an organisation of ideas about one's self which is derived from one's experience with others. Undoubtedly, a positive reality-based concept of self and an awareness of feeling good about oneself is perhaps the most precious quality one can give a child, yet it remains one of the most elusive qualities (Snygg and Combs 1949).

2.2.1 Self-Concept and Disability

The foundations of the self-concept are laid during the early months when the infant begins to delineate himself/herself from the environment through exploration and experience (Broderick and Blewitt 2006). As he/she goes out of the home, he/she learns about the world around him/her and later hears stories from books, radio and television of what children like him/her are doing. Most of these experiences are less assessable to the child with disabilities and development is slower usually than that of a child without disabilities (Sharma et al. 2004). His/her concept of himself/herself, as a separate entity, therefore, is more difficult to achieve from the beginning (Sharma et al. 2004). Being given a name and being addressed by it is a basic part of the development of a concept of oneself (Hardman et al. 1987; Kirk and Gallagher 1983; Meyen 1982; Peterson 1987).

A study examining the social integration and self-concept of students with disabilities in the inclusive classroom was carried out by Cambra and Silvestre (2003). To do this, a sociogram and a self-concept test covering three dimensions: social, personal and academic self-concept, were administered. The study sample was made up of 97 students with special educational needs included in a mainstream school in Catalonia (Spain). These children had hearing, motor, visual, relational, learning and cognitive problems. The results indicated that the students with disabilities had a positive self-concept albeit it was significantly lower than that of their counterparts, especially in the social and academic dimensions.

Studies conducted by Joiner et al. (1989) showed that there is a positive relationship between assertive behaviour and the degree of acceptance of disability among persons with disabilities. Fitchen et al. (1991) included that in everyday social encounters the thoughts and feelings of individuals who are physically disabled were more negative. They also asserted that the mental health too was affected by the poor physique. Elbaum and Sharon (2001) indicated that children with special educational needs tend to have lower self-concept and self-esteem levels than those without disabilities. Ben-Towim and Walker (1995) observed that the development of negative body attitudes may be linked to the emergence of a chronic physical condition during adolescence. Blomquist et al. (1998) further claimed that adolescents with disabilities face considerable barriers such as low expectations from parents and other significant people in the community, a lack of knowledge about career and educational services and poor self-advocacy skills during attempts to achieve their goals. Upadhyay and Tiwari (1985) suggested that when children with disabilities are integrated with children without disabilities, children with disabilities accept their disability yet they have a poor self-concept. Sharma et al. (2004) too reached a similar conclusion that children with disabilities possess a very poor self-concept.

According to Halder and Datta (2012), self-concept has important implications for positive existence, and is a significant variable for achievement in every society. Palmer (2003) too emphasized that self-concept is an important goal for all students with disabilities. Purdie and McCrindle (2004) further established that in Australia the importance of self-concept is highlighted in almost all the statements of the goals of education and is considered as a means of attaining desired outcomes for all students. Recognizing its wider coverage than any other trait of personality self-concept has been chosen for the present investigation for its important implications in general well-being of the adolescents and adults. The literature above indicates that students with disabilities are further vulnerable to the development of a positive self-concept compared to students without disabilities. Therefore, identifying the criticality of the situation addressed students with intellectual disabilities is selected for the present study.

2.2.2 Self-Concept and Intellectual Disability

Children with intellectual disabilities have been included in self-concept research, however, it was often reported that it was difficult to determine accurate results for this population. Stanovich et al. (1998) compared the social integration and academic perceptions of typically developing students (the non-categorised group), students with intellectual disabilities (the group with exceptionalities/disabilities), at-risk students, and students with English as a second language (ESL) in grades 2–8. The non-categorised (typical) group were found to have higher scores in academic self-concept and social acceptance when compared to the exceptional, ESL, and at-risk groups. Similar scores were reported in the academic self-concept for the exceptional, ESL and at-risk groups. For measures of social acceptance, the exceptional group scored lower than all groups and significantly lower than the non-categorised and at-risk groups. However, what needs to be noted here is that the exceptional group included students with learning disabilities and behaviour problems in addition to students with intellectual disabilities; therefore it was not possible to isolate or segregate the results exclusively obtained by the students with diagnosed intellectual disabilities. In the following subsections, self-concept research studies on children, adolescents and adults with intellectual disabilities are outlined.

2.2.2.1 Children with Intellectual Disabilities

In many of the studies on the self-concept of students with intellectual disabilities, up to half of the participants had an IQ score above the accepted upper limit for the mild intellectual disability range (Taylor et al. 1987; Zic and Igrić 2001), or IQ 70 or below (Schalock et al. 2007). Children with mild intellectual disabilities have IQ scores ranging from 50 to 70 and have limits in adaptive abilities and communication skills (American Psychiatric Association 2000). Taylor et al. (1987) found that the students with intellectual disabilities, who were in contact with their typically developing peers for an average of 8.4 h of the school week, were less accepted and more rejected than their matched peers. They also found that their self-concept regarding loneliness and game playing was lower than their matched peers.

Zic and Igric (2001) in their study of 7–10-years old in inclusive Croatian schools found that there was no significant difference in the perception of peer relationships between students with and without intellectual disabilities even though the students with intellectual disabilities were found to be rejected by their peers. Zic and Igric (2001) concluded that the self-concept of the students with intellectual disabilities was less affected by what others thought of them. Since most of the students with intellectual disabilities in the research detailed above had IQ scores higher than 70, the question of whether they can be truly termed as intellectually disabled is dubious.

Donohue (2008) found that children with intellectual disabilities who had lower vocabulary scores tended to have a higher non-academic self-concept. These findings suggested that children with lower cognitive capabilities find that because they do not excel in academic areas, they focus their energy in areas outside of school such as in their physical abilities or socializing with their peers (Donohue 2008). Similar patterns were evidenced in typically developing children by Wiest et al. (1998). They found that children struggling in school became especially skilled in non-academic settings to compensate for what they lacked in academic areas.

Silon and Harter (1985) considered self-concept and self-perceptions to be the product of cognitive processes and, therefore, argued that students with cognitive deficits (i.e. students with intellectual disabilities) were more sensitive towards developing a poor self-concept. Silon and Harter (1985) administered the Perceived Competence Scale for Children (Harter 1982) on children with intellectual disabilities who were between the ages 9 and 12 years and on children without disabilities within that same chronological age. Factorial analysis revealed a pattern which was dissimilar to the factor solution for children without disabilities matched with chronological aged children with intellectual disabilities. Silon and Harter (1985) found similar results for children of pre-school/kindergarten age whose mental age matched with the children with intellectual disabilities. However, children of pre-school/kindergarten age were assessed on the Harter and Pike (1984), a parallel form of the Perceived Competence Scale for Children (Harter 1982). Since it was the parallel form and not the exact form, it might have contained items the meaning of which was different to items contained within the Perceived Competence Scale for Children (Harter 1982), thus questioning the validity of the study which used two different scales on different cohorts to measure the same variable.

Another study was conducted by Cuskelly and Jong (1996) where only the Pictorial Scale of Perceived Competence and Social Acceptance (PPCSA) (Harter and Pike 1984) was administered to children with Down syndrome (developmental age 4–6 years 11 months) and normally developing children of a similar developmental age in Queensland. The results obtained portrayed similar self-concept scores for both groups. However, what needs to be noted here is that students with Down syndrome whose mental age were within the range of 4–6 years 11 months and chronological age within 13–17 years ideally come under the banner of moderate intellectual disabilities. Since participants with moderate intellectual disabilities would have notably low mental ages (4–6 years), to compare them with normally developing children of similar mental ages would mean that very young children/preschoolers (chronological age at least around 4–6 years) were selected in the comparison group and to accurately measure the self-concept of such young children would be difficult.

2.2.2.2 Adolescents with Intellectual Disabilities

Abells et al. (2008) examined the involvement of adolescents with intellectual disabilities in social and recreational activities. Sixty-three parents of high school students with intellectual disabilities completed telephone interviews. The results revealed that students most commonly participated in activities with family members. Fewer adolescents were involved in activities with peers, with the majority of peer activities being organized, around sports. The most common reasons for students not being involved in activities with peers were their disability and lack of available supports. However, the researchers failed to explore the other dimensions of self-concept and examined only the social domain in great detail.

2.2.2.3 Adults with Intellectual Disabilities

Dixon et al. (2006) studied two groups of adults with intellectual disabilities from two institutions. One group were being prepared to move to community living

(Movers) and the other group were staying at their residential setting (Stayers). All of the participants had an IQ within the range of 56–75 for those with mild intellectual disabilities and within the range of 45–56 for those with mild-moderate intellectual disabilities. Multidimensional self-concept was measured by Self Description Questionnaire-III (SDQ-III) (Marsh and Gouvernet 1989) and the Coopersmith Self-esteem Inventory (SEI) (Adult Version) Short Form (1981) was used to assess global self-esteem. Dixon et al. (2006) reported differences on the SDQ-III Academic subscale and SDQ Maths subscale where the Stayers had significantly higher academic self-concept scores than the Movers. In relation to the SDQ Emotion and Physical Ability ($p < 0.05$), the Stayers had higher scores and in the Honesty subscale ($p < 0.05$), the Movers had significantly higher Honesty scores compared to scores for the Stayers (Dixon et al. 2006). According to Dixon et al. (2006), these differences may be accounted for by the differences in mean age between these two groups. They further substantiated that the Academic and Maths subscales could be explained by changes in educational practices for people with mild intellectual disabilities given that younger people have been exposed to more appropriate educational programs in comparison to older people. They further argued that younger people have had less time to lose their academic skills. Similarly, Dixon et al. (2006) claimed that the difference between the Physical Ability subscales could relate to the fact that the participants in Stayers were younger and were all in employment. The descriptive results of the Coopersmith Self-Esteem Inventory (1981) showed that participants with mild intellectual disabilities (even after being exposed to good facilities) had low to average self-esteem compared to the normative groups on this measure, suggesting this as an area worthy of investigation (Dixon et al. 2006).

Duvdevany (2002) compared the self-concept of individuals with intellectual disabilities who participated in integrated recreation activities with non-disabled people and their counterparts who participated in segregated recreation programmes in Israel. The results obtained found that the physical and overall self-concept of individuals with intellectual disabilities who participated in integrated programmes was higher than of those of the individuals who participated in segregated programmes.

Garaigordobil and Pérez (2007) analysed the self-concept and self-esteem of individuals with and without intellectual disabilities and explored whether there were gender differences in these variables in both the groups. The sample included 170 participants aged 19–40, 128 without disability and 42 with intellectual disabilities. The Rosenberg Self-Esteem Scale (RSE; Rosenberg 1965) and the "Listado de adjetivos para la evaluación del autoconcepto en adolescentes y adultos" (LAEA; Garaigordobil, in press) instruments were administered to the subjects. The results revealed that participants with intellectual disabilities scored significantly lower in self-concept and self-esteem than the participants without disabilities; however no significant gender differences were noted in any variables in either of the two groups.

Yet another study, by Li et al. (2006) investigated the self-concept of Chinese adults with intellectual disabilities in Hong Kong. Face-to-face and individual interviews were conducted in Cantonese, using the Chinese version of the Adult Source of Self-Esteem Inventory (ASSEI) (1989) together with three open-ended questions to explore the participants' self-conceptions in different life domains. A sample of 135 adults with intellectual disabilities were interviewed. The findings showed that the family self, the social self and achievement in school and work were the self-concept attributes most important to the participants. The respondents with intellectual disabilities had a higher total self-concept than that of a comparison group of people without disabilities when the participants used the in-group social comparison to maintain positive self-perception. The possible explanation is that almost three quarters of the participants in this study completed special education and most of them were in segregated vocational settings, and thus they were quite likely to adopt the in-group social comparison strategy as suggested by other research studies (Duvdevany 2002).

To summarise, the research studies on participants with intellectual disabilities presented some limitations. Some of the researchers (Taylor et al. 1987; Zic and Igric 2001) in their sample included participants with intellectual disabilities with IQ scores above the accepted upper limit for the mild intellectual disability range. Therefore, there is doubt and suspicion about whether their samples can be truly regarded as representing the diagnosed intellectually disabled. Secondly, while one group of researchers analysed self-concept through a single score (Garaigordobil and Pérez 2007; Silon and Harter 1985), another group investigated self-concept in relation to peer relationships only (Abells et al. 2008; Stanovich et al. 1998; Zic and Igric 2001) and there were yet others who either studied self-concept in relation to physical abilities and social self (Donohue 2008) or attempted to study the family, academic and social self (Li et al. 2006). Only, Tracey and Marsh (2002) and Duvdevany (2002) used the multidimensional self-concept in their studies involving children with mild intellectual disabilities, or in comparing respondents in mainstream and segregated settings. None of the other researchers investigated self-concept in its multi-faceted and varied dimensions in respondents with intellectual disabilities. This research addresses the gap and measures a far greater differentiation of self-concept in relation to the physical, moral, personal, family, social, academic and total self-concepts in students with diagnosed mild intellectual disabilities. In addition, it can be inferred from the literature presented above that research in the area of self-concept in students with intellectual disabilities is still in its embryonic stage. There has been a dearth of research in Australia in relation to the topic concerned, thereby justifying the use of South Australia as the context for the present study.

2.2.3 Impact of School Placement on Self-Concept

Begley (1999) compared the self-concept of students with Down syndrome aged 8–16 years across school placement, age, and sex. No significant difference was attributed to age or sex. Students in mainstream placements generally had more positive self-concepts than students in schools for children with moderate disability. In the Glenn and Cunningham (2001) study which was designed to investigate the usefulness of self-esteem measures with young people (17–24 years) with Down syndrome, the researchers used the Pictorial Scale of Perceived Competence and Social Acceptance for Young Children (PSPCSA) (Harter and Pike 1984) and the Joseph Pre-School and Primary Self-Concept Screening Test (Joseph 1979) to assess the less able participants (mean verbal mental age of 5 years 9 months). The researchers found that the participants did not respond randomly, but seemed to deliberately search for the most positive statement and hence, all rated themselves positively. They concluded that the self-perceived competence of these young people did not match the measures of competence for this population. The participants with higher mental ages (mean verbal mental age of 8 years 9 months) whose self-concept was measured using the Self-Perception Profile for Learning Disabled Students (Renick and Harter 1988), while still reported as having a high self-esteem, appeared to be more realistic in their perception of their competence. Cunningham and Glenn (2004) further claimed that children with intellectual disabilities were particularly susceptible to developing low self-concept due to impaired cognitive ability, stigma, and internalizing negative labels example 'slow' or 'retarded'. Cunningham and Glenn (2004) also found that only individuals with verbal mental ages of eight years and above were able to make the necessary social comparisons to enable them to have a realistic self-concept. These researchers also found that the self-concept of young people with Down syndrome was not affected by experience in mainstream education. They argued that those with higher mental ages were more likely to be attending mainstream classes. They further stated that even those attending special schools would have sufficient contact with mainstream institutions to make the necessary comparisons for establishing self-concept if they were cognitively 'ready' for this. The impact of mainstream educational environments on the self-concept of students with intellectual disabilities clearly needs further investigation because the researchers perceived the mainstream interaction of students with Down syndrome to be contingent on their higher mental age. If higher mental age became the sole factor for positive self-concept and greater mainstream integration for these students, then the question of truly including diagnosed students with intellectual disabilities comes under question and doubt as students with diagnosed intellectual disabilities usually have mental age lower than their chronological age.

Huck et al. (2010) found that children with intellectual disabilities who were included in mainstream classes in Sydney, Australia remained positive at an age when self-concept is likely to be negatively impacted by comparisons with higher performing peers. The researchers conducted their study on children with intellectual disabilities whose mean chronological age was nine years. Participants with intellectual disabilities have lower mental ages as compared to their chronological ages, therefore, in this study it can be inferred that the mean mental age of students with intellectual disabilities must be lower than nine years. As such, it becomes questionable as to how accurately the respondents have answered questions about

difficult concepts such as participants' perceived cognitive competence and perceived peer acceptance. Another limitation of this study was that not all children
were fully included into mainstream classes when the data were collected.

Tracey and Marsh (2002) in a sample of 211 students with mild intellectual
disabilities aged 7–13 years used the Self Description Questionnaire I–Individual
Administration (SDQI-IA) to assess the multidimensionality of participants' self-
concepts and to understand the impact of educational placement (mainstreamed or
non-mainstreamed classes) on children's self-concepts. Confirmatory factor analyses indicated the presence of all eight SDQI-IA factors (average factor load-
ing = 0.80) in their sample of children with mild intellectual disabilities.
Furthermore, correlations between self-concept domains (factors) were low,
indicating that children with mild intellectual disabilities differentiated between
various self-concept areas. Unlike typically developing preadolescents whose
general self-esteem is most highly associated with physical appearance, these
children's general self-esteem was most highly related to their general-school self-
concept according to Tracey and Marsh. They also found that students with mild
intellectual disabilities placed in special classes reported significantly higher
academic self-concepts compared to their counterparts placed in regular classes.
Similar results were obtained by Crabtree (2003) who found that adolescents with
mild intellectual disabilities in special schools had higher academic self-concepts
than adolescents with mild intellectual disabilities in regular schools but that there
was little difference between these groups in terms of non-academic components
of self-concept. Crabtree concluded that "integration does not have its expected
positive effect on self-concept... students integrated into mainstream schools may
face greater levels of stigmatization than those attending special schools" (p. 284).
Contrary to this notion, Marsh et al. (2006) found preadolescents with mild
intellectual disabilities had lower self-concepts in segregated classes than in regular classes for three academic self-concept scales (reading, math and general-
school) and, to a lesser extent, in peer relationships and global self-esteem.
However, similar trends were not observed by these researchers for the other three
non-academic components of self-concept (physical ability, appearance, and parent relationships).

2.2.4 Impact of Stigma on Self-Concept

Research has shown that people with an intellectual disability experience stigma
(Beart et al. 2005; Hastings and Remington 1993). Jahoda et al. (1988) conducted
interviews with 12 adults with intellectual disabilities aged between 21–40 years.
The researchers found that while all participants with intellectual disabilities were
aware of the stigma attached to them, only three regarded themselves as essentially
different from people without intellectual disabilities and held a handicapped view
of themselves.

Perception of stigmatization has been associated with lower self-esteem, self-concept and psychopathology in people with an intellectual disability and in other stigmatized groups (Abraham et al. 2002; Dagnan and Waring 2004; Paterson et al. 2012; Szivos-Bach 1993). Early work by Szivos (1991) with adolescents with intellectual disabilities indicated that those who were most often being stigmatized had the lowest self-esteem. Abraham et al. (2002) also found a negative correlation between self-esteem and perceived stigma in adults with an intellectual disability. Similarly, Dagnan and Waring (2004) noted a significant relationship between the negative evaluations people with an intellectual disability made about themselves and their scores on a measure of stigma perception. They concluded that core negative beliefs about the self are related to the extent to which people feel different (i.e. are aware of stigma) and suggested this may be a result of the group internalizing the stigma they faced. Recent research by Paterson et al. (2012) examined the perception of stigma in adults with an intellectual disability, the relationship this has with their psychological well-being and whether the process of social comparison has a moderating effect on this relationship. The results indicated that perception of stigma was found to be significantly related to negative social comparisons, which in turn strongly related to low self-esteem.

Enhancing self-esteem/self-concept is widely regarded as a desirable goal for the general population, but it is of particular importance for people who have a higher incidence of failure, who lack control of their lives and who may be perceived as vulnerable, such as those with disabilities (Craven et al. 2003; Zetlin and Turner 1988). Persons with intellectual disabilities frequently encounter certain negative experiences (e.g. perceived intellectual inadequacy, a disproportionately high incidence of academic and social failure, social stigmatization and discrimination, unemployment and underemployment) and they are generally viewed as being at risk for low self-concepts (Elbaum and Sharon 2001). Unless self-concept is closely monitored, many interventions and much educational and vocational training effort will be rendered ineffective for this cohort (Marsh and Johnston 1993), making it a critical area for investigation.

References

Abells, D., Burbidge, J., & Minnes, P. (2008). Involvement of adolescents with intellectual disabilities in social and recreational activities. *Journal on Developmental Disabilities, 14*(2), 88–94.

Abraham, C., Gregory, N., Wolf, L., & Pemberton, R. (2002). Self-esteem, stigma and community participation amongst people with learning difficulties living in the community. *Journal of Community and Applied Social Psychology, 12*(6), 430–443. doi:10.1002/casp.695.

American Psychiatric Association. (2000). *Diagnostic and statistical manual of mental disorders: DSM-IV-TR®* (4th ed.). Arlington, VA: American Psychiatric Association.

Beart, S., Hardy, G., & Buchan, L. (2005). How people with intellectual disabilities view their social identity: A review of the literature. *Journal of Applied Research in Intellectual Disabilities, 18*(1), 47–56. doi:10.1111/j.1468-3148.2004.00218.x.

Begley, A. (1999). The self-perceptions of pupils with Down syndrome in relation to their academic competence, physical competence and social acceptance. *International Journal of Disability, Development and Education, 46*(4), 515–529. doi:10.1080/103491299100489.

Ben-Tovim, D. I., & Walker, M. K. (1995). Body image, disfigurement and disability. *Journal of Psychosomatic Research, 39*(3), 283–291. doi:10.1016/0022-3999(94)00143-S.

Blomquist, K. B., Brown, G., Peersen, A., & Presler, E. P. (1998). Transitioning to independence: Challenges for young people with disabilities and their caregivers. *Orthopaedic Nursing, 17*(3), 27–35.

Broderick, P. C., & Blewitt, P. (2006). *The life span: Human development for helping professionals* (2nd ed.). Upper Saddle River, NJ: Pearson, Education Inc.

Cambra, C., & Silvestre, N. (2003). Students with special educational needs in the inclusive classroom: Social integration and self-concept. *European Journal of Special Needs Education, 18*(2), 197–208. doi:10.1080/0885625032000078989.

Coopersmith, S. (1981). *Coopersmith Self-Esteem Inventories*. Mountain View, CA: Consulting Psychologists Press, Inc.

Crabtree, J. W. (2003). Maintaining positive self-concept: Social comparisons in secondary school student with mild learning disabilities attending mainstream and special schools. In H. W. Marsh, R. G. Craven, & D. McInerney (Eds.), *International advances in self research* (Vol. 1, pp. 261–290). Greenwich, CT: Information Age Publishing Inc.

Craven, R. G., Marsh, H. W., & Burnett, P. (2003). Cracking the self-concept enhancement conundrum: A call and blueprint for the next generation of self-concept enhancement research. In H. W. Marsh, R. G. Craven, & D. McInerney (Eds.), *International advances in self research* (Vol. 1, pp. 91–126). Greenwich, CT: Information Age Publishing Inc.

Cunningham, C., & Glenn, S. (2004). Self-awareness in young adults with Down syndrome: Awareness of Down syndrome and disability. *International Journal of Disability, Development and Education, 51*(4), 335–361. doi:10.1080/1034912042000295017.

Cuskelly, M., & Jong, I. (1996). Self-concept in children with Down syndrome. *Down Syndrome Research and Practice, 4*(2), 59–64. doi:10.3104/reports.63.

Dagnan, D., & Waring, M. (2004). Linking stigma to psychological distress: Testing a social–cognitive model of the experience of people with intellectual disabilities. *Clinical Psychology and Psychotherapy, 11*(4), 247–254. doi:10.1002/cpp.413.

Dixon, R. M., Craven, R., & Martin, A. (2006). *The measurement of multidimensional self-concept in adults with mild intellectual disability*. Paper presented at the Self-concept, motivation, social and personal identity for the 21st Century: Proceedings of the 4th International Biennial SELF Research Conference, Ann Arbor, University of Michigan.

Donohue, D. K. (2008). *Self-concept in children with intellectual disabilities*. Master of Arts (Psychology Theses. Paper 46), Georgia State University, Atlanta. Available in http://digitalarchive.gsu.edu.proxy.library.adelaide.edu.au/psych_theses/46.

Duvdevany, I. (2002). Self-concept and adaptive behaviour of people with intellectual disability in integrated and segregated recreation activities. *Journal of Intellectual Disability Research, 46*(5), 419–429. doi:10.1046/j.1365-2788.2002.00415.x.

Elbaum, B., & Sharon, V. (2001). School-based interventions to enhance the self-concept of students with learning disabilities: A meta-analysis. *The Elementary School Journal, 101*(3), 303–329. doi:10.2307/1002249.

Fitchen, Adler, Agam, & Severson, (1991). Reaction of parents and siblings of disabled individuals towards the disability, their attitude and coping behaviour. *Individual Psychology, 46*(3), 324–357.

Franken, R. E. (1994). *Human motivation* (3rd ed.). Pacific Grove, CA: Brooks/Cole Publishing Co.

Garaigordobil, M., & Perez, J. I. (2007). Self-concept, self-esteem and psychopathological symptoms in persons with intellectual disability. *Spanish Journal of Psychology, 10*(1), 141–150.

Glenn, S., & Cunningham, C. (2001). Evaluation of self by young people with Down syndrome. *International Journal of Disability, Development and Education, 48*(2), 163–177. doi:10.1080/10349120120053649.

Halder, S., & Datta, P. (2012). An exploration into self concept: A comparative analysis between the adolescents who are sighted and blind in India. *British Journal of Visual Impairment, 30*(1), 31–41. doi:10.1177/0264619611428202.

Hardman, M. L., Drew, C. J., & Egan, M. W. (1987). *Human exceptionality: Society, school, and family* (2nd ed.). Boston: Allyn and Bacon.

Harter, S. (1982). The perceived competence scale for children. *Child Development, 53*(1), 87–97.

Harter, S., & Pike, R. (1984). The pictorial scale of perceived competence and social acceptance for young children. *Child Development, 55*(6), 1969–1982.

Hastings, R. P., & Remington, B. (1993). Connotations of labels for mental handicap and challenging behaviour: A review and research evaluation. *Mental Handicap Research, 6*(3), 237–249. doi:10.1111/j.1468-3148.1993.tb00055.x.

Huck, S., Kemp, C., & Carter, M. (2010). Self-concept of children with intellectual disability in mainstream settings. *Journal of Intellectual and Developmental Disability, 35*(3), 141–154. doi:10.3109/13668250.2010.489226.

Jahoda, A., Markova, I., & Cattermole, M. (1988). Stigma and the self-concept of people with a mild mental handicap. *Journal of Intellectual Disability Research, 32*(2), 103–115. doi:10.1111/j.1365-2788.1988.tb01396.x.

Joiner, J. G., Lovett, P. S., & Goodwin, L. K. (1989). Positive assertion and acceptance among persons with disabilities. *Journal of Rehabilitation, 55*(3), 22–29.

Joseph, J. (1979). *Pre-school and primary self-concept screening test.* Wood Dale, IL: Stoelting Co.

Kirk, S. A., & Gallagher, J. J. (1983). *Educating exceptional children* (4th ed.). Boston: Houghton-Mifflin.

Li, E. P.-Y., Tam, A. S.-F., & Man, D. W.-K. (2006). Exploring the self-concepts of persons with intellectual disabilities. *Journal of Intellectual Disabilities, 10*(1), 19–34. doi:10.1177/1744629506062270.

Marsh, H. W., & Gouvernet, P. J. (1989). Multidimensional self-concepts and perceptions of control: Construct validation of responses by children. *Journal of Educational Psychology, 81*(1), 57–69. doi:10.1037/0022-0663.81.1.57.

Marsh, H. W., & Johnston, C. F. (1993). Multidimensional self-concepts and frames of reference: Relevance to the exceptional learner. In F. E. Obiakor & S. W. Stile (Eds.), *Self-concept of exceptional learners: Current perspectives for educators* (pp. 72–112). Dubuque, Iowa: Kendall/Hunt Publishing Company.

Marsh, H. W., Tracey, D. K., & Craven, R. G. (2006). Multidimensional self-concept structure for preadolescents with mild intellectual disabilities: A hybrid multigroup–MIMC approach to factorial invariance and latent mean differences. *Educational and Psychological Measurement, 66*(5), 795–818. doi:10.1177/0013164405285910.

Meyen, E. L. (1982). *Exceptional children and youth, an introduction* (2nd ed.). Denver, CO: Love Publishing Co.

Palmer, C. D. (2003). *Social competence of children with albinism.* Unpublished Ph.D. thesis, The University of Queensland, Queensland.

Paterson, L., McKenzie, K., & Lindsay, B. (2012). Stigma, social comparison and self-esteem in adults with an intellectual disability. *Journal of Applied Research in Intellectual Disabilities, 25*(2), 166–176. doi:10.1111/j.1468-3148.2011.00651.x.

Peterson, N. L. (1987). *Early intervention for handicapped and at-risk children: An introduction to early childhood-special education.* Denver, CO: Love Pub. Co.

Purdie, N., & McCrindle, A. (2004). Measurement of self-concept among Indigenous and non-Indigenous Australian students. *Australian Journal of Psychology, 56*(1), 50–62. doi:10.1080/00049530410001688128.

Purkey, W. (1988). An overview of self-concept theory for counsellors. *ERIC Digest*, 1–6. Retrieved from http://files.eric.ed.gov/fulltext/ED304630.pdf

Renick, M. J., & Harter, S. (1988). *Manual for the self-perception profile for learning disabled students*. Denver, CO: University of Denver.

Rosenberg, M. (1965). *Society and the adolescent self-image*. Princeton, NJ: Princeton University Press.

Schalock, R. L., Luckasson, R. A., Shogren, K. A., Borthwick-Duffy, S., Bradley, V., Buntinx, W. H., et al. (2007). The renaming of mental retardation: Understanding the change to the term intellectual disability. *Intellectual and Developmental Disabilities, 45*, 116–124.

Sharma, N., Vaid, S., & Jamwal, Z. (2004). The concept of self in physically challenged institutionalized children. *Disability India Journal*.

Silon, E. L., & Harter, S. (1985). Assessment of perceived competence, motivational orientation, and anxiety in segregated and mainstreamed educable mentally retarded children. *Journal of Educational Psychology, 77*(2), 217–230.

Snygg, D., & Combs, A. W. (1949). *Individual behaviour: A new frame of reference for psychology*. New York: Harper.

Stanovich, P. J., Jordan, A., & Perot, J. (1998). Relative differences in academic self-concept and peer acceptance among students in inclusive. *Remedial and Special Education, 19*(2), 120–126. doi:10.1177/074193259801900206.

Szivos, S. E. (1991). Social comparisons with siblings made by adolescents with a learning difficulty. *Journal of Community and Applied Social Psychology, 1*(3), 201–212. doi:10.1002/casp.2450010303.

Szivos-Bach, S. E. (1993). Social comparisons, stigma and mainstreaming: The self esteem of young adults with a mild mental handicap. *Mental Handicap Research, 6*(3), 217–236. doi:10.1111/j.1468-3148.1993.tb00054.x.

Taylor, A. R., Asher, S. R., & Williams, G. A. (1987). The social adaptation of mainstreamed mildly retarded children. *Child Development, 58*(5), 1321–1334.

Tracey, D. K., & Marsh, H. W. (2002). Self-concepts of preadolescents with mild intellectual disability: Multidimensionality, measurement, and support for the big fish little pond effect. *Self-Concept Research: Driving International Research Agendas, 35*, 419–427.

Upadhyay, S. N., & Tiwari, K. R. (1985). Role of socio-economic status in frustration and anxiety. *Scientia Paedagogica Experimentalis, 22*(1), 109–114.

Wiest, D. J., Wong, E. H., & Kreil, D. A. (1998). Predictors of global self-worth and academic performance among regular education, learning disabled, and continuation high school students. *Adolescence, 33*(131), 601–618.

Zetlin, A. G., & Turner, J. L. (1988). Salient domains in the self-conception of adults with mental retardation. *Mental Retardation, 26*(4), 219–222.

Zic, A., & Igrić, L. (2001). Self-assessment of relationships with peers in children with intellectual disability. *Journal of Intellectual Disability Research, 45*(3), 202–211. doi:10.1046/j.1365-2788.2001.00311.x.

Chapter 3
Theoretical Background

Abstract This chapter outlines the evolution of the term 'self' and how it has been used and defined by different psychologists, sociologists over the course of many decades. The multidimensional structure of self-concept substantiated by many researchers is highlighted. The self-concept framework employed in this study is identified. This is a viable and tested framework which can be operationalized for the collecting and analysing of self-concept data from the students with intellectual disabilities which is the focus of this study. An overview of specific theories to understand how the self-concept functions in the experience of students with disabilities are discussed.

Keywords Self · Structure of self-concept · Multidimensional self-concept · Social comparison theory · Big fish little pond theory · Labelling theory

3.1 Introduction to Self-Concept

One of the most complex terms found in psychology is 'self' (Rosenberg 1989). The exact time of its origin is still unknown. In early periods, it was the province of philosophers, and was fostered for many years under their care. To them it was a phenomenon of subjective realization that is, the realization of the soul and beyond sensory claims (Castell 1965).

However, being liberated from philosophical thought it became of interest to psychologists, sociologists and many others and in the wave of modern psychology, the term 'self' began to be viewed as an observable measurable phenomenon (Rosenberg 1989). Therefore, Rosenberg (1989) claimed that the manner in which different psychologists defined it became more realistic but not fully detached from subjective experience. In order to evolve an operational meaning to the term, as well as to understand the developmental background of the subject, a theoretical framework for the analysis of self-concept needs to be provided.

P. Datta, *Students with Intellectual Disabilities*, SpringerBriefs in Education,
DOI: 10.1007/978-981-287-017-9_3, © The Author(s) 2014

According to Jung (1915) the 'self' is an archetype which develops during mid-childhood and represents the reconciliation and fusion of opposites, the Conscious (CS) and the Unconscious (UCS). Jung argued that the self is the centre of personality, providing stability and equilibrium. It does not develop until the other aspects of the personality are developed and individualized. By 'self' Adler (1930) means a subjective system which allows experiences to become meaningful for the individual and provides a framing to seek experiences which will fulfil the person's life style. The self, it is argued, gives meaning to life, creating the goal of life as well as helping to fulfil it. Sullivan (1953) defined self as the concept of self system. This suggests a secondary dynamism dissociated from the rest of the personality, the organisation of which controls awareness. This analysis includes the personified self, as well as the process by which anxiety provoking experiences and perceptions are kept from awareness. Alternatively, Rogers (1959), purports that 'the self' is the portion of the personality which consists of perceptions of 'I' or 'me' and develops out of the organism's interaction with the environment. The developing 'self' strives for consistency, interjects the value of others which may be perceived in a distorted way, and changes as a result of maturation of learning.

James (1890) wrote extensively about the self as an object of knowledge. According to him 'self' is that which a person considers part of or representing himself or herself. He argues that there are many selves representing an individual, such as the material self, the social self and the spiritual self. Cooley (1902) suggested that people perceive themselves as they might perceive their image in a mirror and in fact he described this conception as the 'looking-glass self'. Later, Freud (1945) adopted the term 'ego' to refer to this organized aspect of personality and numerous other theorists have adhered to this usage. In Warren's (1962) Dictionary of Psychology, 'self' is defined as an individual regarded as conscious of his/her own continuing identity and of his/her relation to his/her environment.

On the basis of the above definitions the term 'self' will be used in this study to mean traits and characteristics which make up the individual and consists of perceptions of 'I' or 'Me', as defined by William James (1890). The self is not the sudden outburst of the traits or characteristics of an individual. It follows a process of development and gradually unfolds itself through certain stages (Loevinger 1966), and is continually in a state of evolution.

3.2 The Structure of Self-Concept

Historically, self-concept has been examined as a uni-dimensional construct comprising a general or overall self-concept. Coopersmith (1967, p. 6) claimed that "children make little distinction about their worthiness in different areas of experience or, if such distinctions are made, they are made within the context of the overall, general appraisal of worthiness that the children have already made". Over a decade later Marx and Winne (1978) also concluded that "self-concept seems more of a unitary concept than one broken into distinct sub-parts or facets", as cited in Craven and Yeung (2008, p. 270). Research utilising a uni-dimensional model of self-concept typically demonstrated self-concept across a range of general contexts representing a single score based on an average of the total score of items measuring self-concept, supposed to reflect an individual's sense of self across the various areas of his or her life.

The validity of the one-dimensional model has been seriously challenged in later years and criticised by researchers who advocate that self-concept is a multidimensional construct (Harter 1990; Little et al. 1990; Marsh 1988; Marsh and Gouvernet 1989). Over the past decade a substantial amount of research on construct validity, led by Marsh and his colleagues (Marsh and Hattie 1996), have demonstrated self-concept to be multidimensional (Byrne 1984; Marsh and Gouvernet 1989). Studies conducted with adolescents with mild disabilities have also successfully identified multiple self-concept facets for these students (Little et al. 1990). Self-concept theorists have argued that a general score often masks or veils important distinctions that individuals make about their competence and capabilities in different dimensions of their lives (Harter 1990). "This agglomerate use of general self-concept is particularly dubious and probably led to many of the contradictory findings which abound in self-concept research" (Marsh 1988, p. 40).

In an effort to remedy some of these deficiencies, Shavelson et al. (1976) developed a hierarchical, multifaceted model of self-concept. They proposed a highly influential theoretical view of the self that has received further research confirmation (Byrne and Shavelson 1996). Shavelson et al. (1976) described self-concept as a person's perceptions of self formed through attributions of one's own behaviour, influenced by interactions with significant others and experience with one's environment. In this model children's general self-concept is represented as two main domains: academic and non academic self-concepts. Academic self-concept is further divided into specific school subject areas such as mathematics, science, English and social studies. The non-academic self-concept is divided into social, emotional and physical self-concepts. This last domain is further subdivided into physical ability and physical appearance (Broderick and Blewitt 2006, pp. 212–213). The Marsh and Shavelson (1985) model also indicates that the non-academic self-concept is divided into physical ability, physical appearance, peer relationships and parent relationships, emphasizing the multi-dimensionality of self-concept. Figure 3.1 illustrates the multi-faceted model of self-concept adapted from Marsh and Shavelson (1985).

Fitts and Warren (1996) developed the Tennessee Self-Concept Instrument to confirm the multi-faceted structure of self-concept. This has been employed successfully by a number of researchers over the last decade in their studies involving students with intellectual disabilities. Duvdevany (2002) studied the many dimensions of self-concept in individuals with intellectual disabilities in mainstream and segregated settings. Tracey and Marsh (2002) also confirmed the multidimensionality of self-concept in children with mild intellectual disabilities. These researchers developed a far greater differentiation of self-concept compared to the Shavelson et al. (1976) and Marsh and Shavelson (1985) models. These research studies confirmed that students with intellectual disabilities, much like

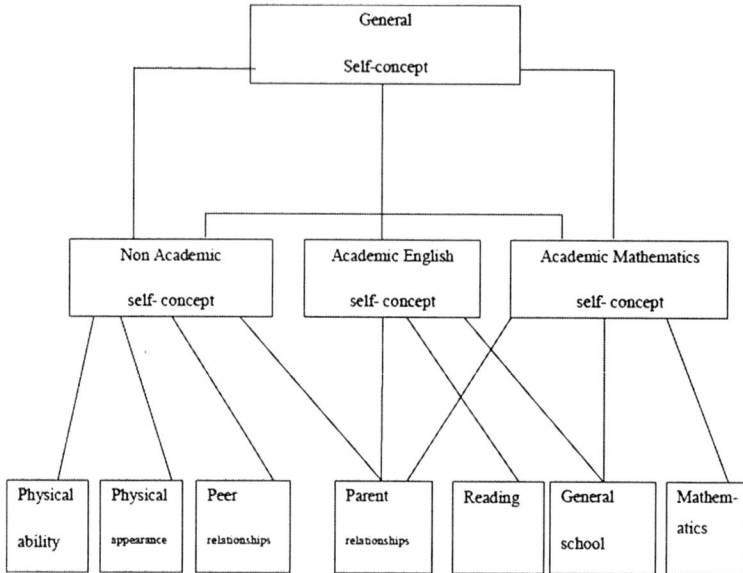

Fig. 3.1 Self-concept: Its multifaceted, hierarchical structure (Adapted from Marsh and Shavelson 1985, p. 114)

their non-disabled peers, were able to differentiate and hold views on the diverse and varied dimensions of self-concept. In view of the recognition, acceptance and inclusion of the different and multiple dimensions of self-concept, the Tennessee Self-Concept instrument, as streamlined and updated by Fitts and Warren (2003), was employed in this research to measure self-concept across its different dimensions in students with intellectual disabilities.

The Tennessee Self-Concept instrument (2003) measures the non-academic self-concept with particular reference to Physical, Moral, Personal, Family and Social dimensions. The test includes an additional Academic/Work score that tells how respondents see themselves in school and job settings. It does not measure outcomes in the form of different school subjects. Therefore, the Tennessee self-concept questionnaire measures the different dimensions of self-concept that were derived largely from the Shavelson et al. (1976) model, the Marsh and Shavelson (1985) model and other recent research studies. These dimensions of self-concept are the basis of this research and have been identified as the themes under which the questionnaire and interview responses were analysed. The interview analysis also followed these themes in the questions raised in the interviews.

Specific theories to understand how the self-concept functions in the experience of students with disabilities are discussed in the following sections.

3.3 Social Comparison Theory

In recent years, social comparison theory has emerged as a highly regarded theory in self concept formation. According to this theory, one's self-concept is largely determined by the ways in which one perceives or comprehends significant others in the environment. The origin of research interest in social comparison processes can be attributed to Festinger (1954), who noted that there seems to be a strong impetus in most individuals to assess and appraise their opinions and abilities against an established standard. In the absence of some definite and explicit objective criteria, people usually identify and compare with others in the environment as the basis for forming subjective estimates of their personal ability levels and self-worth. Festinger (1954) maintained that individuals need to compare themselves to others in order to define the self, and then pass judgement on their verdict. In this way, individuals use others in their immediate environment as the basis for forming comparative subjective judgments of self worth (Festinger 1954). The perceived similarity between two individuals increases the likelihood of them comparing their capabilities with one another. People usually select similar others as a basis of social comparison when faced with a choice between relatively similar and dissimilar people. It is thought that social comparison processes are affected by the particular reference group the individual is employing.

Social comparison theory (Gibbons 1986; Szivos-Bach 1993), speculates that people with disabilities living in the community will make comparisons with other non-disabled groups and it is likely that their self-concept will decrease because of negative frames of reference effects. Research based on social comparison theory emphasises that, in situations where the self-concept is in jeopardy, there are three possibilities: people may minimise or limit comparisons (Brickman and Bulman 1977), avoid upward comparisons (Steil and Hay 1997) or try to self-enhance by engaging in downward comparisons (Crocker et al. 1987). In situations where the self-concept is endangered people may prefer to compare themselves with inferior others. This may result in an enhancement in self-concept and an increase in subjective well-being because of employing downward comparisons (Gibbons 1986).

Veroff (1969) indicated that young children are not able to spontaneously exercise social comparison information, as Festinger's theory would suggest, until after the early years of schooling. Ruble, Boggiano, Feldman and Loebl (1980) found that self-evaluations of children at different age levels did not employ social comparison feedback until at least 7 years of age. Research has substantiated that preschool children do not use social comparison for self-appraisal because they find it difficult and complex (Ruble 1983; Veroff 1969). Therefore, the social comparison theory comes into play during and after late childhood, through adolescence and adulthood, which were the chosen stages for the sample collected for this study.

3.4 Big Fish Little Pond Theory

The big fish little pond effect, based on social comparison theory, anticipates that students with mild disabilities have higher academic self-concepts when they are placed in a special class of other students with disabilities as they are able to compare themselves with parallel, mediocre or inferior others. The big fish little pond effect states that individuals have a tendency to compare themselves with others around them when forming their self-concept. Therefore, it is likely that if students with mild disabilities are placed in regular classes with peers without disabilities who perform better academically, then the self-evaluations and appraisals of students with mild disabilities will be adversely affected, and their academic self-concept abridged (Marsh 1984). As intellectual dimension is the only criterion to have its frame of reference related to placement in regular or special classes, it follows that the negative effects of regular classes are limited primarily to the academic components of self-concept and the damage is substantially smaller for non-academic (e.g. social, physical) components of self-concept.

3.5 Labelling Theory

The Labelling theory, in contrast to the social comparison and big fish little pond theories, predicts that students with mild disabilities when placed in special classes with other students with mild disabilities have lower self-concepts. Labelling theory argues that the identification, isolation and segregation of these students in separate placements produces alienation, stigmatisation and a sense of deviance, and thereby fosters a negative self-concept (Goffman 1963). This theory also anticipates that placement in a special class has adverse or negative effects, particularly on the general self-concept and is likely to influence both academic and non-academic components of self-concept. According to Stobart (1986), labelling and stigmatisation are seen to occur most often when students are placed in special classes as a result of their disability diagnosis. This claim has been widely supported by many other researchers who have argued that applying labels to children and segregating and excluding them from the mainstream school population results in stigmatisation and a concomitant reduction in self-concept (Burbach 1981; Cole and Meyer 1991; Guskin et al. 1975; Thomas 1997).

References

Adler, A. (1930). *The education of children*. London: George Allen and Unwin.
Brickman, P., & Bulman, R. J. (1977). Pleasure and pain in social comparison. In J. M. Suls & R.
    L. Miller (Eds.), *Social comparison processes: Theoretical and empirical perspectives* (pp.
    149–186). Washington, DC: Hemisphere.

Broderick, P. C., & Blewitt, P. (2006). *The life span: Human development for helping professionals* (2nd ed.). Upper Saddle River, NJ: Pearson, Education Inc.

Burbach, H. J. (1981). The labelling process: A sociological analysis. In J. M. Kauffman & D. P. Hallahan (Eds.), *Handbook of special education* (pp. 361–377). Englewood Cliffs, NJ: Prentice-Hall.

Byrne, B. M. (1984). The general/academic self-concept nomological network: A review of construct validation research. *Review of Educational Research, 54*(3), 427–456. doi:10.3102/00346543054003427.

Byrne, B. M., & Shavelson, R. J. (1996). On the structure of social self-concept for pre-, early, and late adolescents: A test of the Shavelson, Hubner, and Stanton (1976) model. *Journal of Personality and Social Psychology, 70*(3), 599–613. doi:10.1037/0022-3514.70.3.599.

Castell, A. (1965). *The self in philosophy.* New York: MacMillan.

Cole, D. A., & Meyer, L. H. (1991). Social integration and severe disabilities: A longitudinal analysis of child outcomes. *Journal of Special Education, 25*(3), 340–351. doi:10.1177/002246699102500306.

Cooley, C. H. (1902). *Human nature and the social order.* New York: C. Scribner's Sons.

Coopersmith, S. (1967). *The antecedents of self-esteem.* San Francisco: W. H. Freeman.

Craven, R. G., & Yeung, A. S. (2008). Advances in self-concept theory, research and intervention. In D. M. McInerney & A. D. Liem (Eds.), *Teaching and learning: International best practice* (Vol. 8, pp. 269–294). Charlotte, NC: Information Age Publishing Inc.

Crocker, J., Thompson, L. L., McGraw, K. M., & Ingerman, C. (1987). Downward comparison, prejudice, and evaluations of others: Effects of self-esteem and threat. *Journal of Personality and Social Psychology, 52*(5), 907–916. doi:10.1037/0022-3514.52.5.907.

Duvdevany, I. (2002). Self-concept and adaptive behaviour of people with intellectual disability in integrated and segregated recreation activities. *Journal of Intellectual Disability Research, 46*(5), 419–429. doi:10.1046/j.1365-2788.2002.00415.x.

Festinger, L. (1954). A theory of social comparison processes. *Human Relations, 7*(2), 117–140. doi:10.1177/001872675400700202.

Fitts, W. H., & Warren, W. L. (1996). *Tennessee Self-concept Scale* (2nd ed.). Los Angeles, CA: Western Psychological Services.

Fitts, W. H., & Warren, W. L. (2003). *Tennessee self-concept scale manual* (2nd ed.). Los Angeles, CA: Western Psychological Services.

Freud, A. (1945). Indications for child analysis. *Psychoanalytic Study of the Child, 1*, 127–149.

Gibbons, F. X. (1986). Social comparison and depression: Company's effect on misery. *Journal of Personality and Social Psychology, 51*(1), 140–148. doi:10.1037/0022-3514.51.1.140.

Goffman, E. (1963). *Stigma: Notes on the management of spoiled identity.* Englewood Cliffs, NJ: Prentice-Hall.

Guskin, S., Bartel, N., & MacMillan, D. (1975). Perspective of the labeled child. In N. Hobbs (Ed.), *Issues in the classification of children: A sourcebook on categories, labels and their consequences* (Vol. 2, pp. 189–212). San Francisco, CA: Jossey-Bass Publishers.

Harter, S. (1990). Issues in the assessment of the self-concept of children and adolescents. In A. M. L. Greca (Ed.), *Through the eyes of the child: Obtaining self-reports from children and adolescents* (pp. 292–325). Boston, MA: Allyn and Bacon.

James, W. (1890). The principles of psychology *Encyclopedia Britannica* Chicago. Retrieved from http://www.britannica.com/EBchecked/topic/476946/The-Principles-of-Psychology.

Jung, C. G. (1915). *The theory of psychoanalysis.* New York: The Journal of Nervous and Mental Disease Publishing Company.

Little, T., Widaman, K., Farren, A., MacMillan, A., Hemsley, R., & MacMillan, D. (1990). *The factor structure and reliability of the Self Description Questionnaire (SDQII) in an early adolescent population, stratified by academic level, ethnicity and gender.* Riverside: University of California, School of Education.

Loevinger, J. (1966). The meaning and measurement of ego development. *American Psychologist, 21*(3), 195–206. doi:10.1037/h0023376.

Marsh, H. W. (1984). Self-concept: The application of a frame of reference model to explain paradoxical results. *Australian Journal of Education, 28*(2), 165–181.

Marsh, H. (1988). *Self Description Questionnaire 1: A theoretical and empirical basis for the measurement of multiple dimensions of preadolescent self-concept: A test manual and a research monograph.* San Antonio, TX: Psychological Corporation.

Marsh, H. W., & Gouvernet, P. J. (1989). Multidimensional self-concepts and perceptions of control: Construct validation of responses by children. *Journal of Educational Psychology, 81*(1), 57–69. doi:10.1037/0022-0663.81.1.57.

Marsh, H. W., & Hattie, J. (1996). Theoretical perspectives on the structure of self-concept. In B. A. Bracken (Ed.), *Handbook of self-concept: developmental, social, and clinical considerations* (pp. 38–90). New York: Wiley.

Marsh, H. W., & Shavelson, R. (1985). Self-concept: Its multifaceted, hierarchical structure. *Educational Psychologist, 20*(3), 107–123.

Rogers, C. R. (1959). A theory of therapy, personality, and interpersonal relationships as developed in the client-centered framework. In S. Koch (Ed.), *Psychology: A study of a science* (Vol. III, pp. 184–256)., Formulations of the person and the social context New York: McGraw-Hill.

Rosenberg, M. (1989). Self-concept research: A historical overview. *Social Forces, 68*(1), 11–34. doi:10.1093/sf/68.1.34.

Ruble, D. N. (1983). The development of social comparison processes and their role in achievement-related self-socialization. In E. T. Higgins, D. N. Ruble, & W. W. Hartup (Eds.), *Social cognition and social development: A socio-cultural perspective* (pp. 134–157). New York: Cambridge University Press.

Ruble, D. N., Boggiano, A. K., Feldman, N. S., & Loebl, J. H. (1980). Developmental analysis of the role of social comparison in self-evaluation. *Developmental Psychology, 16*(2), 105–115. doi:10.1037/0012-1649.16.2.105.

Shavelson, R. J., Hubner, J. J., & Stanton, G. C. (1976). Self-concept: Validation of construct interpretations. *Review of Educational Research, 46*(3), 407–441.

Steil, J. M., & Hay, J. L. (1997). Social comparison in the workplace: A study of 60 dual-career couples. *Personality and Social Psychology Bulletin, 23*(4), 427–438. doi:10.1177/0146167297234008.

Stobart, G. (1986). Is integrating the handicapped psychologically defensible? *Bulletin of the British Psychological Society, 39,* 1–3.

Sullivan, H. S. (1953). *The interpersonal theory of psychiatry* (1st ed.). New York: W.W. Norton.

Szivos-Bach, S. E. (1993). Social comparisons, stigma and mainstreaming: The self esteem of young adults with a mild mental handicap. *Mental Handicap Research, 6*(3), 217–236. doi:10.1111/j.1468-3148.1993.tb00054.x.

Thomas, G. (1997). Inclusive schools for an inclusive society. *British Journal of Special Education, 24*(3), 103–107. doi:10.1111/1467-8527.00024.

Tracey, D. K., & Marsh, H. W. (2002). Self-concepts of preadolescents with mild intellectual disability: Multidimensionality, measurement, and support for the big fish little pond effect. *Self-Concept Research: Driving International Research Agendas, 35,* 419–427.

Veroff, J. (1969). Social comparison and the development of achievement motivation. In C. P. Smith (Ed.), *Achievement-related motives in children* (pp. 46–101). New York: Russell Sage Foundation.

Warren, H. C. (Ed.). (1962). *Dictionary of psychology, 1934/1962 (renewed).* Cambridge: The Riverside Press.

Chapter 4
Methodology and Research Methods

Abstract This chapter delineates the research methods adopted for the two stages of this study. The research questions act as starting points to design an appropriate methodology, which in turn influences the selection of strategies suitable for data collection and generation. Qualitative methodology which is exploratory or interpretative in nature is identified for this study. The use of the methods namely survey questionnaire and interviews are explained and justified in a meaningful way. The pilot study undertaken to test the appropriateness and robustness of the research methods is provided. Finally, the procedure and rigor adopted for administration, respondent recruitment and data analysis for the main study is described in great detail.

Keywords Qualitative methodology · Survey questionnaires · Interviews · The pilot study · Respondent recruitment · Data analysis

4.1 Introduction

Research methods according to Crotty (1998, p. 3) are "the techniques or processes used to gather or analyse data related to some research question or hypothesis", while the notion of methodology "constitutes the link between the paradigm-related questions and the methods (O'Donoghue 2007, p. 12). Methodology is "the strategy, plan of action, process or design lying behind the choice and use of particular methods and linking the choice and use of methods to the desired outcomes" (Crotty 1998, p. 3). In this study, the methodology employed was qualitative and the methods used were survey questionnaire and interviews.

P. Datta, *Students with Intellectual Disabilities*, SpringerBriefs in Education,
DOI: 10.1007/978-981-287-017-9_4, © The Author(s) 2014

4.2 The Qualitative Methodology

According to Palmer (2003, p. 96), "qualitative methodology enables researchers to collect richer data, greater density of information, more vivid description and clarity of meaning that generally cannot be acquired through quantitative measures". She stated that "qualitative research methods recognise the multiple realities of situations and interpretations, and their quality and character depend on the circumstances in which the research is conducted" (p. 96). Unlike quantitative research methods, which rely on the accumulation of facts and their translation into numbers, qualitative research identifies and describes (Palmer 2003).

Qualitative research is often exploratory or interpretative in nature. Qualitative methods illuminate, explain, and interpret rather than verify. Burns (2000) claims that the "qualitative mode of inquiry is characterised by methodological eclecticism, a hypothesis free orientation and an implicit acceptance of the natural scheme of things" (p. 13). He went on to say that qualitative research involves methods of enquiry that can play an important role in examining relationships, suggesting causes and effects, and evaluating dynamic processes in school settings. In other words, qualitative research enables a deeper understanding, "an insider's view of the field" (p. 13). The strength of qualitative research is that the quality of the participants' responses is examined, rather than just the response itself. Burns also states, "qualitative methods can highlight subtleties in pupil behaviour and response, illuminate reasons for action and provide in-depth information on interpretation" (p. 13). In methods such as interviews, interaction between the investigator and participants occurs, providing the researchers with a clearer picture of the subject's perspective, and enabling them to "construct social reality [and to] focus on interactive processes" (Neuman 2000, p. 16), and consider the "changing nature of reality" (Guray 1989, p. 5). "Qualitative research is a form of systematic empirical inquiry into meaning" (Shank 2006, p. 5). Shank (2006) argues that qualitative research is any form of inquiry that depends upon the world of experience in some fundamental way. He further claims that the qualitative researcher develops a "rich, deep, thick, textured, insightful and best of all illuminative picture of the phenomenon or situation" (p. 5). Qualitative methodology was chosen for this research because it is a good way to tap into participant's thoughts and experiences to understand them. This research was guided by the interpretative approach. "Interpretation is a productive process that sets forth the multiple meanings of an event, object, experience, or text" (Denzin and Lincoln 1998, p. 322). Interpretation is illuminative; it throws light on the respondents' experiences (Denzin and Lincoln 1998). Seen in this light, the qualitative researcher's task is to understand these experiences.

4.3   Research Procedures and Methods

This research was divided into two stages of execution. In Stage 1, survey questionnaire was administered to students with intellectual disabilities to determine the scores of self-concept and its dimensions. In Stage 2 of this research, interviews were conducted with students with intellectual disabilities, their parents and their teachers to provide insights into what these students were able to achieve in the different dimensions of self-concept and the reasons for high or low self-concept of these students.

4.3.1   Survey Questionnaires

According to Creswell (2008), survey designs are procedures in which the researcher administers a survey or questionnaire to a small group of people (called the sample) to identify trends in attitudes, perceptions, behaviours or characteristics of a large group of people (called the population). In this procedure, survey researchers collect numbered data using questionnaires and analyse the data to describe trends about responses to questions and to test research questions or hypotheses (Creswell 2008). They also interpret the meaning of the data by relating results of the statistical test back to past research studies (Creswell 2008).

4.3.2   Interviews

A qualitative interview occurs when the researcher asks one or more participants general, open-ended questions and records their answers. The researcher then transcribes and types the data into a computer file for analysis (Creswell 2008). Open-ended questions allow participants to voice their experiences unconstrained by any perspectives of the researcher or past research findings (Creswell 2008). Such semi-structured interviews allow "greater depth than is the case with other methods of data collection" (Cohen and Manion 1989 as cited in O'Donoghue 2007, p. 133). Interviewing has a wide variety of forms. The most common type of interviewing is individual, face-to-face verbal interchange (Denzin and Lincoln 1998) which was used in this study for students with intellectual disabilities and teachers. However, interview can take the form of mailed or self-administered questionnaires (Denzin and Lincoln 1998) which was also used in this study for all parents.

4.4 The Pilot Study

A pilot study was conducted on students with intellectual disabilities in South
Australia prior to the major data collection to test the appropriateness and
robustness of the survey questionnaire namely the Tennessee self-concept Questionnaire. The purpose of the pilot was to establish whether the questionnaire in its
existing form was appropriate to the respondents. This followed the procedure
adapted by Palmer (2003) for her social competence study of students with albinism, students with vision impairments but not albinism, and students with no
vision problems. It was found that students with mild intellectual disabilities
comprehended and easily responded to the questions asked in the survey and
therefore, the survey questionnaire was found suitable and appropriate to be
administered to students with mild intellectual disabilities in South Australia.

The questions on the interview protocol were also trialled with people known
to the researcher in order to refine questioning techniques and question structure
prior to the formal interviews beginning, a technique also recommended by
O'Donoghue (2007). To ensure that no emotional discomfort was experienced by
any of the students, parents and teachers, the survey questionnaire and the
interview questions were piloted with all three groups to identify potential
problems. In the administration of the interview question on the social self-
concept, teachers considered it inappropriate for students to be asked "Who do
you like or dislike and why"? This approach could encourage students to think
negatively about peers. As a result, a more appropriate form of the question was
substituted, and students were asked "Who do you like to mix with and why"?

The survey questionnaire and the interview questions were also checked by
active researchers from two universities and vetted by professionals from the field
of special education. Participants in the pilot study were informed of their right not
to answer questions that caused them discomfort.

4.5 The Main Study

In Stage 1 of this project, the use of the questionnaire was appropriate to provide
answer to the first research question stated in Chap. 1. The Tennessee self-concept
questionnaire was administered to determine the self-concept scores across the
dimensions and the total self-concept of the students with intellectual disabilities.
From this students with low and/or high self concept scores could be identified.
Questionnaire data provided the basis for further and subsequent qualitative
exploration.

Questionnaires and interviews can be successfully combined when the former
reveals that "deeper exploration of the subject is necessary" (Kaufman et al. 2006,
p. 115). Hence, the purpose of Stage 2 interviews with specific students with
intellectual disabilities, their parents and teachers was to understand why the

self-concept was low or high in the students under study. In Stage 2, the remaining research question stated in Chap. 1 was answered by conducting interviews with the three groups of respondents. Multiple interviews enabled the researcher to collect data from a range of viewpoints and to examine the last research question from different perspectives.

4.6 Stage 1 Survey Questionnaire

Stage 1 involved the administration of Tennessee self-concept questionnaire developed by Fitts and Warren (2003) to students with intellectual disabilities.

4.6.1 Tennessee Self-Concept Scale (TSCS:2)

The Tennessee self-concept Scale: Second Edition (TSCS:2) has been updated and streamlined by Fitts and Warren (2003) to provide researchers and clinicians with materials that are easy to use, yet which retain the characteristics that have given the test such a wide appeal over the past several decades. Although inefficient and outdated items have been eliminated and scoring procedures have been simplified, most of the original items have been retained and the obtained scores are psychometrically equivalent to their counterparts in the 1988 edition. An Academic/Work self-concept scale has been added. In addition, the TSCS: 2 have been re-standardized on a nationwide sample of over 3,000 individuals ranging in age from 7 to 90 years old. There are two forms of the TSCS: 2- The Adult Form and the Child Form. The Adult Form has 82 items and the Child Form has 76 items. Both forms consist of self-descriptive statements that allow the individual to portray his or her own self-picture using five response categories-'Always False', 'Mostly False', 'Partly False and Partly True', 'Mostly True' and 'Always True'. The forms can be administered individually or in groups, and can be completed in 10–20 min. The Adult Form is standardized on 1,944 individuals aged 13–90 (Fitts and Warren 2003). The TSCS:2 Adult Form is appropriate for adolescents in high school and for adults (ages 13 and older) and therefore, only the Adult Form version of the questionnaire has been used in this research as the age range of the students in this study was between 15 and 25 years. The Adult Form can be completed by individuals who can read at approximately a third-grade level or higher (Thomas et al. 1975 as cited in Fitts and Warren 2003). The Flesch Reading Easy Score for the Adult Form is 89 % (Flesch 1979) indicating very easy reading hence quite suitable to be administered to students with mild intellectual disabilities. The basic scores are the six self-concept scores namely Physical, Moral, Personal, Family, Social and Academic/Work and the summary score i.e. the total self-concept score. The external scales—Physical, Moral, Personal, Family, and Social—are similar to the traits posited on many subsequent instruments (Marsh and Shavelson 1985). Four Validity Scores for examining response bias within the Tennessee self-concept questionnaire are Inconsistent Responding, Self Criticism, Faking Good and Response Distribution. Over the course of many years of development and use, the Tennessee self-concept Scale (TSCS: 2) has been found to produce reliable and valid results (Fitts and Warren 2003). It has been shown to be reliable across time, have internally consistent scales and reflect coherent personal attributes (Fitts and Warren 2003). It is valid both when compared to other accepted psychological instruments and when distinguishing among various groups (Fitts and Warren 2003). The internal consistency estimates for the TSCS: 2 Adult Form scores range from .73 to .95. The test-retest reliability and the validity scores for the TSCS: 2 Adult Form is 0.82 and 0.31 respectively (Fitts and Warren 2003).

4.6.2 Administration

Each individual student was provided with the Tennessee self-concept questionnaire. The administration setting was comfortable, well lighted, ventilated and free from noise and other distractions as possible. The questionnaire was administered to the students with intellectual disabilities on a one-on-one basis. The students were directed to fill in the demographic information and the date, and to read the instructions carefully. The researcher ensured that the instructions were carefully understood by the respondents. There was no time limit for the questionnaire, although respondents were discouraged from spending a great deal of time on any one item. Participants were instructed to provide only one answer to each item, and if unsure, to answer according to what was most generally and recently true for them. Since the administration was on a one-to-one basis, the researcher ensured that students responded to all the items. When administering the questionnaire to students, the researcher read the directions aloud while the students read them silently. If questions arose during the administration session, the researcher's response was supportive but noncommittal, for example, 'Please give the answer that best describes how you generally feel'.

The total time estimated to fill out the Tennessee self-concept questionnaire by the students with intellectual disabilities was 45 minutes. Upon completion, questionnaires were collected by the researcher to maintain student confidentiality. The Information Sheet and Consent Form for the adult students with mild intellectual disabilities were provided in simple language and the research project was explained to them by the researcher in the presence of a witness. For students with intellectual disabilities, the items on the Tennessee self-concept questionnaire was read aloud by the researcher wherever they needed it as administration was on a one-on-one basis. Participation by students was purely voluntary and confidentiality was strictly maintained.

4.6.3 Respondent Recruitment

This study used the Purposive Sampling method, which is a kind of non-probability sample based upon the typicality of the cases to be included in the sample (Singh 2006). The researcher considers that the sample selected is a very good representative of the population. Singh (2006, p. 352) explains that the researcher identifies the participants in such a way that the selected sample yields as quickly as possible the same averages and proportions as the totality has with respect to the characteristics to be studied. The purposeful sampling technique is defined as "researchers intentionally selecting individuals and sites to learn or understand the central phenomenon" (Creswell 2003, p. 204). Data collection was conducted in mainstream and specialist schools and Technical and Further Education (TAFE) Institutes in South Australia. The schools and TAFE Institutes were contacted by the researcher via telephone or e-mail. A letter outlining the research along with the University of Adelaide and Department for Education and Child Development (DECD) previously known as Department of Education and Children's Services (DECS) Ethics approval documents were sent to the Principal. The names and the contact details of the students were accessed through school and institute records with prior permission obtained from the Principal. Some of the adult students with intellectual disabilities were contacted via organisations that provided support to people with intellectual disabilities. Names and addresses were forwarded by the organisations when permission for participation in the study was provided by the participant. Students (above 18 years) were given the Information Sheet and Consent Forms personally by the researcher and the purpose of the study was explained to them. The researcher personally collected the Consent Forms from students (above 18 years) where consent was given freely. If necessary, the researcher read and explained the documents to the student in the presence of a witness to ensure that they understood the nature and requirements of the project in order to obtain informed student consent. For students below 18 years, the Information Sheet and Consent Form were provided to their parents/guardians/care givers either through the students carrying it to their homes or by post (the pack included self addressed paid envelopes as well). Similarly, the Consent Forms were returned to the researcher in a manner that the students bought it back to the school from where the researcher collected it or it was mailed directly to the researcher by the parents. The questionnaires were administered to students during school and institute working hours in their premises. All students who participated in Stage 1 of the study were clearly informed that their details would be kept strictly confidential. A good rapport was established between the research participants and the researcher during the administration of questionnaires. They were informed that they were able to withdraw at any time during the research project and assurance was provided to the students that their abrupt withdrawal would not affect their academic performance or their position in the school/institution.

4.6.4 The Participants

In this study, adolescent and adult students with only mild intellectual disabilities were included. Adolescent and adult students with moderate, severe and profound intellectual disabilities were excluded as it would be difficult for them to comprehend the items in the questionnaires and answer independently.

A total of 20 students with mild intellectual disabilities completed the Tennessee self-concept questionnaire. The student samples were matched in terms of the following characteristics:

- Age—age range between 15–18 years for the adolescent students and between 19–25 years for the adult students;
- Education level—Year 9–12 for the adolescent students and full time vocational courses for the adult students;
- Schools—there are three sectors of education in South Australia namely the Catholic Education System, Association of Independent Schools of South Australia (AISSA) and Department for Education and Child Development (DECD). Technical and Further Education (TAFE) is one of the post school options in South Australia. This study focussed only on the schools run by DECD and the TAFE Institutes because both are owned and operated by the Government of South Australia.

The range of students (adolescents and adults) according to gender is presented in Table 4.1.

4.6.5 Data Analysis

Each completed questionnaire was given a number for identification purposes and to ensure confidentiality. This comprised the prefix ID (for students for intellectual disabilities), followed by a number from 1 to 20 according to the chronological order of questionnaire collection (ID-1, ID-2 etc.). The entire analytical process for self-concept was according to the Tennessee self-concept Manual and attested by the supervisory panel that moderate this research. The overview of students with intellectual disabilities for Stage 1 questionnaire responses is outlined in Table 4.2.

4.6.6 Scoring Instructions

The Tennessee self-concept questionnaire was hand scored. A desk calculator was helpful. The scoring instructions for the questionnaire based on the Tennessee self-concept manual (Fitts and Warren 2003) are outlined in the following subsections.

Table 4.1 Students according to gender

	Male	Female	Total
Adolescent + adult students with intellectual disabilities	10	10	20

Table 4.2 Overview of students with intellectual disabilities for stage 1 responses (questionnaire data)

Background	Gender		Age		Stage	
	Male	Female	15–18	19–25	Adolescents	Adults
Number of respondents	10	10	10	10	10	10

4.6.6.1 Tennessee's Self-Concept Questionnaire

The scoring procedure for the four validity scores namely Inconsistent Responding, Faking Good, Response Distribution and Self-Criticism and the seven self-concept scores namely the Physical, Moral, Personal, Family, Social, Academic and the Total self-concept scores are presented below.

To determine the Inconsistent Responding (INC) raw score, the response values for each item pair were entered in the spaces provided. Then, the absolute value of the difference in response values (i.e. the sample size of the difference, regardless of which response value is larger) was entered in the 'Difference' spaces provided. The INC raw score is the sum of these differences. That number was entered in the space provided for the INC raw score on the Profile Sheet.

Inconsistent Responding (INC) Score

Item 1 _____ and Item 69 _____ = _____

Item 3 _____ and Item 65 _____ = _____

Item 6 _____ and Item 44 _____ = _____

Item 7 _____ and Item 20 _____ = _____

Item 9 _____ and Item 43 _____ = _____

Item 10 _____ and Item 77 _____ = _____

Item 13 _____ and Item 15 _____ = _____

Item 21 _____ and Item 58 _____ = _____

Item 29 _____ and Item 30 _____ = _____

INC Raw Score: _____

To calculate the Faking Good (FG) raw score, for each item specified below the response value was copied into the space provided. Then it was calculated as directed. The result was transferred to the space provided for the FG raw score on the Profile Sheet.

Faking Good (FG) Score

(_____ + _____ + _____ + _____ + _____) – (_____ + _____) = _____

Item 1   Item 3   Item 21   Item 22   Item 64   Item 28   Item 41   FG Raw Score

To determine the Response Distribution (RD) raw score, the number of 1s and 5s were counted on the Scoring Worksheet for all items. This number was entered in the space provided for the RD raw score on the Profile Sheet.

To calculate the remaining raw scores, the Scoring Worksheet was referred. Each item's response value was copied into the boxes in the same row. The numbers in each column was added and the subtotals in the spaces provided at the bottom of each page were recorded. The column subtotals from the first page of the Worksheet was transferred to the designated spaces at the bottom of the second page. The two subtotals for each column were added to obtain the raw score for that scale. The raw scores to the spaces provided at the bottom of the Profile Sheet were transferred. The spaces provided at the bottom of the second page of the Scoring Worksheet were used to calculate the Total (TOT) raw score. The TOT raw score is the sum of the Physical, Moral, Personal, Family, Social and Academic/Work raw scores.

The participant's TSCS: 2 T-scores was obtained by plotting all the raw scores recorded on the Profile Sheet. T-scores are standard scores with a mean of 50, and a standard deviation of 10. Thus a T-score below 40 on any scale falls at least one standard deviation below the mean, and a T-score above 60 falls at least one standard deviation above the mean.

To obtain T-scores for the TSCS: 2 scales, a mark was placed and located over the raw score for each scale in the appropriate column on the Profile Sheet. The T-score that correspond to the obtained raw score value for each scale can be found along the left and right margins of the Profile Sheet, in the same row where the raw score appeared. The T-score for each scale was entered in the spaces provided at the bottom of the Profile Sheet. A copy of the TSCS: 2 Scoring Worksheet and TSCS: 2 Profile Sheet are attached in Appendices A and B, respectively.

4.7 Stage 2 Interviews

As previously stated, Stage 1 was the backgrounding phase used to gain information on the basic dimensions of the topic being investigated and to help determine the self-concept scores. Stage 2 interviews were conducted to provide insights into the questionnaire responses, and to delve deeper into the reasons for the low and/or high self-concept of the students. This is in line with Gillham's thinking who states that "any research which aims to achieve an understanding of people in a real world context is going to need some interview material, if only to provide illustration, some insight into what it is like to be a person in that setting" (Gillham 2000, p. 12).

4.7.1 Interview Design

The interview questions were developed to find answer to the overarching last research question stated in Chap. 1. The questions on the interview protocol were developed that centred on the broad themes namely 'Physical self-concept', 'Moral self-concept', 'Personal self-concept', 'Family self-concept', 'Social self-concept' and 'Academic/Work self-concept'. The six themes have been derived from the Tennessee self-concept questionnaire in the analysis of the questionnaire data. The interview questions for the three groups of participants were to ensure that the problem under investigation was thoroughly examined and the themes explored. The interviews with the students and teachers were face to face and semi-structured. Interviews were audio-taped, and notes taken to enable the researcher to draw inferences about the self-concepts of the students with intellectual disabilities. In order to be consistent, an 'interview protocol' was considered useful and designed as a guide that contains instructions for the process of interviews to be taken place, questions to be asked and space created to take notes of the responses (Creswell 2008).

All parents were sent interview questions to their e-mail or mailing address (they preferred this way) which they answered and returned to the researcher either through e-mail or in the self-addressed envelope provided in the pack. Electronic e-mail or mail interviews are also useful in collecting qualitative data quickly from a geographically dispersed group of people (Creswell 2008).

For the qualitative elements of this research, the researcher chose to perform face-to-face (Denzin and Lincoln 1998; Gillham 2000) and semi-structured (Kvale 1996) interviews with the students and teachers. The primary reason for choosing a face-to-face approach was that questions relating to self-concept could be sensitive in nature and trust therefore played an important role (Gillham 2000) which could not have been established in a non face-to-face interview. In the same way, there were a number of reasons for choosing a semi-structured approach. The semi-structured interview method allowed participants to answer on their own terms more than a fully structured interview would have permitted. They were encouraged to elaborate on questions in order to provide more comprehensive descriptions on self-concept.

	Teachers	Parents	Adolescent + adult students with intellectual disabilities	Total
Table 4.3 The range and numbers of participants who agreed to be interviewed	4	5	9	18

4.7.2 Participant Recruitment

Stage 1 students were invited to participate in an interview. When the students with intellectual disabilities (above 18 years) and parents returned the Consent Forms in Stage 1, students (above 18 years) indicated for themselves and parents indicated on behalf of their children and for themselves whether they wanted to participate in an interview at a later date. Some declined for personal reasons. Teachers from those schools and institutes where students participated in Stage 1 were given the Information Sheet and Consent Forms personally by the researcher and the purpose of the study was explained to them. The researcher personally collected the Consent Forms from teachers where consent was given freely. Only those teachers were selected for this study who had students with intellectual disabilities in their classes. The times were arranged to interview teachers and students within the business hours of the school or institute in its premises. A warm and close rapport was established between the research participants and the researcher during the interview process. Parents who returned signed consent forms were contacted by telephone, briefed about the study and interview questions were sent to their mailing address. All packages sent out to parents in their mailing address contained paid self-addressed envelopes inside which parents returned their interview responses to the researcher.

Out of the twenty students with intellectual disabilities in Stage 1, nine students volunteered to be interviewed. Four teachers and five parents agreed to be interviewed. Table 4.3 presents the range and number of participants who agreed to be interviewed.

4.7.3 Developing Rapport

The student and the teacher interviews were conducted on a one-on-one basis in the school or institute during working hours. A casual and relaxed atmosphere was deliberately encouraged and interviews took a primarily conversational tone (Kvale 1996). The researcher was mindful of signs of impatience, annoyance and boredom, but such gestures never surfaced. The level of interest by both parties proved to be valuable and aided in the subsequent fluidity of the transcription process. In that sense, the interview was a process of constructing a shared narrative to which the researcher, students and teachers contributed. All parents were sent the interview questions to their mailing address; however prior to this rapport was also established with them through telephonic conversations.

4.7.4   Voice Recordings

To avoid the distractions and background noise, interviews with students with intellectual disabilities and teachers were conducted in private exclusive rooms within the schools/institute. Interviews were recorded (with participants permission) with a digital recorder and batteries were changed every couple of interviews, not only to ensure the voice data were recorded, but to make certain that time was not wasted and rapport was maintained. The digital recorder was later connected to the personal computer and laptop of the researcher and copies were saved in electronic Windows Media Player (.mp3) format.

4.7.5   Interview Narratives

Interviews generated a substantial amount of data as the participants talked about the self-concept across the various dimensions. The duration of each interview was typically 45 min to an hour long and yielded between 2,000 and 8,000 words of transcript each. Personally transcribing the voice data provided the ideal opportunity to commence the process of analysis, as the files needed to be frequently replayed in the transcription process.

Transcripts differ in their precision (Velliaris 2010). It is often difficult to get down on paper exactly what was said. There is also the issue of whether (or how) to include grammatical errors, digressions, abrupt changes of focus, exclamations, and other indications of mood, such as laughter and tears. A considered judgement may conclude that for most projects, transcripts do not need to be this perfect (Rubin and Rubin 2005).

The more the researcher listened to the tapes and read the personal comments, the more she became familiar with each text and began to construct categories and recognize common patterns. The hermeneutic back-and-forth checking was constant within and between interviews. The first draft transcriptions represented an attempt to faithfully and reliably transcribe every word in the order it was spoken. A copy of the transcribed versions of the interviews was sent to the relevant interviewees (teachers and students) at the earliest possible convenience to ensure data compatibility and dependability, a technique suggested by Poland (1995). This measure was undertaken to reduce the potential for loss and distortion that can occur when transcribing (Cohen et al. 2000) and importantly, to reaffirm that the texts were suitable and acceptable for continued inclusion in this research. The opportunity for participants in this study to review and amend transcribed comments prior to its completion, further secured the validity of the interview responses. Any changes made during this process (and these were only few), resulted in the second and final version of the transcripts.

4.7.6 Interview Data Analysis

Each interviewee was given a number for identification purposes. Among the students with intellectual disabilities that completed the Stage 1 questionnaires, some of them chose to participate in Stage 2 interviews. These students with intellectual disabilities had the same code (ID-1, ID-2 etc.) in Stage 2 as they were coded in Stage 1. Teachers and parents that participated in Stage 2 were denoted as T (for teachers) and P (for parents) followed by an alphabet. Teachers of students with intellectual disabilities are coded T-e to T-h. Parents of students with intellectual disabilities are coded P-f to P-j. For greater ease and clarity when interpreting the data, numerals were used for students with intellectual disabilities and alphabetic letters were used for teachers and parents. The interview analysis followed the themes in the questions raised in the interviews.

Data were thematically united and the researcher adopted an iterative approach to ascertain relationships among the responses; similarities and differences in the form of excerpts and expressions. Rather than looking for meaning(s) in discrete words, the researcher concentrated on pools of information and in this way, issues of credibility were addressed by making the analysis as contextual as possible. According to Denzin and Lincoln (1998), in qualitative research there are two types of interpreters: people who have actually experienced what has been described, and those who are often ethnographers or field-workers, so-called well-informed experts. In this study, the students with intellectual disabilities, their parents and teachers described these students' experiences in self-concepts. Although the researcher has no personal experience of being intellectually disabled, she has background knowledge and experience in working with students with special educational needs and disabilities which has enabled her to interpret the data in a systematic social scientific way. The entire analytical process was a personal endeavour validated by the research project supervisory panel.

4.8   Ethical Considerations

The appropriate documents for the University of Adelaide Ethics Committee's approval, and also the Department for Education and Child Development (DECD) (previously known as Department of Education and Children's Services [DECS]) ethics approval for this project had been obtained. Participation in the study was strictly on a voluntary basis. Participants were informed that they could discontinue involvement at any time during the study. Confidentiality was a high priority at all times, and personal information regarding the nature of the intellectual disability and the participants' perceptions about the different dimensions of students' self-concept were recorded and stored safely.

Participants were informed of their right to refuse to answer questions that made them feel uncomfortable. Participants were also informed that the interview would be discontinued if participants showed evidence of emotional distress and only continued if the interviewer believed that to do so would not lead to further discomfort.

References

Burns, R. B. (2000). *Introduction to research methods* (4th ed.). London; Thousand Oaks, CA: Sage Publications.

Cohen, L., Manion, L., & Morrison, K. (2000). *Research methods in education* (5 ed.). London; New York: Routledge.

Creswell, J. W. (2003). *Research design: Qualitative, quantitative, and mixed method approaches* (2nd ed.). Thousand Oaks, CA: Sage Publications.

Creswell, J. W. (2008). *Educational research: Planning, conducting, and evaluating quantitative and qualitative research* (3rd ed.). Upper Saddle River, NJ: Pearson/Merrill Prentice Hall.

Crotty, M. (1998). *The foundations of social research: Meaning and perspective in the research process*. St Leonards: Allen and Unwin.

Denzin, N. K., & Lincoln, Y. S. (1998). *Collecting and interpreting qualitative materials*. Thousand Oaks, CA: Sage Publications.

Fitts, W. H., & Warren, W. L. (2003). *Tennessee self-concept scale manual* (2nd ed.). Los Angeles, CA: Western Psychological Services.

Flesch, R. (1979). *How to write plain English: A book for lawyers and consumers*. New York: Harper & Row.

Gillham, B. (2000). *Research interview*. London; New York: Continuum International Publishing Group.

Guray, C. (1989). *Focus group methodology: An exploration of qualitative research*. Sydney: New South Wales Medical Education Project.

Kaufman, R. A., Guerra, I., & Platt, W. A. (2006). *Practical evaluation for educators: Finding what works and what doesn't*. Thousand Oaks, CA: Corwin.

Kvale, S. (1996). *Interviews: An introduction to qualitative research interviewing*. Thousand Oaks, CA: Sage Publications.

Marsh, H. W., & Shavelson, R. (1985). Self-concept: Its multifaceted, hierarchical structure. *Educational Psychologist, 20*(3), 107–123.

Neuman, W. L. (2000). *Social research methods: Qualitative and quantitative approaches* (4th ed.). Boston: Allyn and Bacon.

O'Donoghue, T. (2007). *Planning your qualitative research project: An introduction to interpretivist research in education*. Milton Park, Abingdon, OX: Routledge.

Palmer, C. D. (2003). *Social competence of children with albinism*. Unpublished Ph.D. thesis, The University of Queensland, Queensland.

Poland, B. D. (1995). Transcription quality as an aspect of rigor in qualitative research. *Qualitative Inquiry, 1*(3), 290–310. doi:10.1177/107780049500100302.

Rubin, I. S., & Rubin, H. J. (2005). *Qualitative interviewing: The art of hearing data*. Thousand Oaks, CA: Sage Publications.

Shank, G. D. (2006). *Qualitative research: A personal skills approach* (2nd ed.). Upper Saddle River, NJ: Pearson Merrill Prentice Hall.

Singh, A. K. (2006). *Tests, measurements and research methods in behavioural sciences*. New Delhi: Bharti Bhavan.

Velliaris, D. M. (2010). *International parents in Tokyo and the education of their transnational children*. Doctoral thesis, University of Adelaide, Australia. Retrieved from http://digital.library.adelaide.edu.au/dspace/handle/2440/63326

Chapter 5
Analysis of Stage 1 Data: Tennessee Self-Concept Questionnaire

Abstract This chapter reports and analyses the self-concept survey questionnaire data for the female and male students with intellectual disabilities. The self-concept analysis is undertaken on the basis of the Tennessee Self-Concept Manual (Fitts and Warren 2003) and follows the six dimensions namely Physical, Moral Personal, Family, Social and Academic Self-Concepts and thus, Total Self-Concept. In addition, the four validity scores namely Inconsistent Responding (INC), Self-Criticism (SC), Faking Good (FG) and Response Distribution (RD) for all students with intellectual disabilities are also provided. The findings reveal that while the majority of the students with intellectual disabilities obtained low scores in Physical, Moral, Personal, Family, Social, Academic and Total Self-Concepts, half of the female students with intellectual disabilities obtained average that is normal scores in Family, Social and Academic Self-Concepts.

Keywords Physical self-concept · Moral self-concept · Personal self-concept · Family self-concept · Social self-concept · Academic self-concept

5.1 Introduction

The aim in administering questionnaires, namely the Tennessee Self-Concept questionnaire to students with intellectual disabilities was to determine the scores of self-concept and its dimensions (physical, moral, personal, family, social, academic and total self-concept) of the individuals under investigation. In Stage 1, twenty students with intellectual disabilities (10 females and 10 males) completed the questionnaires. The entire analytic process employed in interpreting the questionnaire data on self-concept was based on the Tennessee Self-Concept Manual developed by Fitts and Warren (2003). The self-concept analysis followed the six dimensions used in the Tennessee Self-Concept Manual namely Physical Self-Concept, Moral Self-Concept, Personal Self-Concept, Family Self-Concept, Social Self-Concept and Academic Self-Concept and thus, Total Self-Concept. Individuals with Physical, Moral, Personal, Family, Social, Academic and Total

P. Datta, *Students with Intellectual Disabilities*, SpringerBriefs in Education, DOI: 10.1007/978-981-287-017-9_5, © The Author(s) 2014

Table 5.1 Overview of
T-scores for Inconsistent
Responding

Female I.D. (N = 10)	Male I.D. (N = 10)
56	80
56	46
46	42
42	42
59	32
54	54
54	46
50	42
37	56
54	33

I.D. Students with intellectual disabilities

Self-Concept scores less than or equal to 40T are regarded as low, between 41T to 59T are average (normal), greater than or equal to 60T are high and beyond 70T are considered to be very high (Fitts and Warren 2003). In addition, four validity scores namely Inconsistent Responding (INC), Self-Criticism (SC), Faking Good (FG) and Response Distribution (RD) for all students with intellectual disabilities were explored based on the Tennessee Self-Concept Manual. The validity scores are designed to identify defensive, guarded, socially desirable, or other unusual or distorted response patterns (Fitts and Warren 2003). The conversion from raw scores to T-scores for each of the students in the entire analysis has been according to the Tennessee Self-Concept Manual.

For anonymity purposes, as stated in Chap. 4, each student was provided a numeric for identification purposes, comprising the prefix ID (for students with intellectual disabilities) followed by a number (ID-1). In the sections that follow, the four validity scores, the scores on the six dimensions and the Total Self-Concept from the Tennessee Self-Concept Manual of the students with intellectual disabilities are discussed in detail.

5.2 Inconsistent Responding

The Inconsistent Responding (INC) score indicates "whether there is an unusually wide discrepancy in the individual's responses to pairs of items with similar content-pairs of items such as 'I am an attractive person' and 'I look fine just the way I am'. Such a discrepancy is often due to haphazard or careless responding. It may, on the other hand, reflect some peculiarity in the individual's life circumstances that is referred to by the content of particular item pairs" (Fitts and Warren 2003, p. 15). In either case, unusually high INC scores greater than or equal to 70T indicate that an individual's TSCS: 2 profile should be interpreted with caution (Fitts and Warren 2003). Table 5.1 presents the T-scores for Inconsistent Responding for the female and male students with intellectual disabilities:

Table 5.2 Overview of
T-scores for Self-Criticism

Female I.D. (N = 10)	Male I.D. (N = 10)
53	42
42	55
45	39
42	45
31	45
41	38
41	51
38	41
41	37
45	45

I.D. Students with intellectual disabilities

Table 5.1 indicates that 100 % of the female students with intellectual disabilities and 90 % of the male students with intellectual disabilities obtained INC scores below 70T. The remaining 10 % of the male students with intellectual disabilities scored INC scores greater than 70T.

INC scores below 70T indicate that the students' response patterns are consistent and considered to be valid (Fitts and Warren 2003). Therefore, the responses of the great majority of students with intellectual disabilities in this study are reliable and valid.

5.3 Self-Criticism

The items that contribute to the Self-Criticism (SC) score "are all mildly derogatory statements, such as 'I get angry sometimes'—common frailties that most people would admit to when responding candidly" (Fitts and Warren 2003, p. 15). If the SC score is 40T or lower, it means that the individual denies most of these statements and thus obtains such a low score is being defensive and making a deliberate effort to present a favourable picture of himself or herself (Fitts and Warren 2003). A low SC score is a sign that further investigation, perhaps through interview questions or study of the respondents, should be initiated (Fitts and Warren 2003).

A score between 40T and 70T, on the other hand generally indicates a normal, healthy openness and capacity for self-criticism (Fitts and Warren 2003). A high SC score, near the upper boundary of the normal limits may reflect an actual predominance of maladaptive behaviours, such as rudeness, lying or excessive irritability, and it signals an unusual candour or dwelling on personal faults (Fitts and Warren 2003). Table 5.2 presents the T-scores for Self-Criticism for the female and male students with intellectual disabilities.

Table 5.3 Overview of T-scores for Faking Good	Female I.D. (N = 10)	Male I.D. (N = 10)
	45	45
	51	42
	42	45
	48	36
	59	33
	33	29
	36	27
	44	36
	36	32
	36	42

I.D. Students with intellectual disabilities

Table 5.2 indicates that 80 % of the female students with intellectual disabilities and 70 % of the male students with intellectual disabilities obtained SC scores between 40T and 70T. The remaining 20 % of the female students with intellectual disabilities and 30 % of the male students with intellectual disabilities scored SC scores below 40T.

To sum up, in line with Fitts and Warren (2003) it can be interpreted that students who obtained SC scores between 40T to 70T are not trying to appear unusually positive or negative in their self-description. On the other hand, as stated by Fitts and Warren (2003), students with SC scores lower than 40T are somewhat defensive in their self-description. A low SC score does not, of course, prove 'faking good', because the rare angelic individual may be describing his or her typical behaviour (Fitts and Warren 2003). Finally, students with high SC scores beyond 70T tend to focus more on their failings. It means that these students are unusually willing to highlight their personal faults. These students are highly candid individuals (Fitts and Warren 2003).

5.4 Faking Good

Stanwyck and Garrison (1982) as cited in Fitts and Warren (2003) developed the Faking Good (FG) score by requesting that college students deliberately 'fake good' as if they were applying for a fictitious job and wished to present a favourable impression. The items that best discriminated between student responses in the faking condition and those of students given the standard instructions were selected to contribute to the FG score. These items included statements such as 'I have a healthy body' and 'I consider myself a sloppy person'. Thus, "the scale is an indicator of the tendency to project a falsely positive self-concept" (Fitts and Warren 2003, p. 20). A FG score of 70T or above indicates a possibly invalid protocol (Fitts and Warren 2003). Table 5.3 presents the T-scores for Faking Good for the female and male students with intellectual disabilities.

Table 5.4 Overview of T-scores for Response Distribution

Female I.D. (N = 10)	Male I.D. (N = 10)
65	48
50	21
36	26
26	30
40	26
31	29
29	30
35	31
28	34
30	21

I.D. Students with intellectual disabilities

Table 5.3 indicates that 100 % of the female students with intellectual disabilities and 100 % of the male students with intellectual disabilities also obtained FG scores below 70T.

The FG scores of the students, according to Fitts and Warren (2003) do not indicate a conscious attempt to present themselves in an unusually positive and favourable light and thus are valid.

5.5 Response Distribution

The Response Distribution (RD) score is calculated by counting the number of extreme responses circled by the individual. This score is highly correlated with the pattern of the individual's responses as distributed across all five available response options for each TSCS: 2 item. It is interpreted as a measure of certainty about the way one sees oneself. A high RD score greater than or equal to 60T indicates that the individual is very definite in describing himself or herself, whereas a low score less than or equal to 40T reveals the opposite (Fitts and Warren 2003).

An extremely high RD score greater than or equal to 70T may indicate a stereotyped or polarized set of responses. Individuals with extremely high RD scores have chosen a large number of 'Always False' or 'Always True' responses. They do not show much of the typical qualifying or tempering of responses that is usually found. Instead they show either extreme definiteness of response or almost a flippant and impulsive response pattern (Fitts and Warren 2003). Table 5.4 presents the T-scores for Response Distribution for the female and male students with intellectual disabilities.

Table 5.4 indicates that 20 % of the female students with intellectual disabilities and 10 % of the male students with intellectual disabilities obtained RD

Table 5.5 Overview of
T-scores for Physical
self-concept

Female I.D. (N = 10)	Male I.D. (N = 10)
38	34
41	35
47	36
36	34
38	32
32	29
32	32
32	32
32	30
37	34

I.D. Students with intellectual disabilities

scores between 40T and 60T. The remaining 90 % of the male students with intellectual disabilities scored RD scores below 40T. Out of the remaining 80 % of the female students with intellectual disabilities, 70 % scored below 40T and 10 % scored above 60T; however, below 70T.

Students who obtained RD scores between 40T and 60T are in the average range, according to Fitts and Warren (2003). The findings presented above indicate that the responses of these students are not unusually extreme. It can be interpreted according to the Manual of Fitts and Warren (2003) that students who obtained RD scores below 40T are being defensive and guarded and avoid committing themselves by employing the 'Partly False and Partly True' response. By not committing to either 'Mostly True' or 'Mostly False' responses for large numbers of items, these students are showing indecision or extreme guardedness. Students who obtained RD scores above 60T; however, below 70T reflect a somewhat higher level of certainty than is expressed by most people (Fitts and Warren 2003).

5.6 Physical Self-Concept

The Physical Self-Concept (PHY) scale contains items such as 'My body is healthy' (positively scored) and 'I am a sick person' (negatively scored). The PHY score presents "the individual's view of his or her body, state of health and the individual's perception of maintaining a healthy lifestyle" (Fitts and Warren 2003, p. 23). Table 5.5 presents the T-scores for Physical self-concept for the female and male students with intellectual disabilities.

Table 5.5 indicates that 80 % of the female students with intellectual disabilities and 100 % of the male students with intellectual disabilities obtained low PHY scores (below 40T). The remaining 20 % of the female students with intellectual disabilities scored PHY scores in the average range (above 40T and below 50T).

Table 5.6 Overview of
T-scores for Moral
self-concept

Female I.D. (N = 10)	Male I.D. (N = 10)
42	32
42	41
41	47
39	32
42	29
31	27
29	28
29	28
28	36
31	36

I.D. Students with intellectual disabilities

5.7 Moral Self-Concept

The Moral Self-Concept (MOR) scale contains items such as 'I think I do the right thing most of the time' (positively scored) and 'I shouldn't tell so many lies' (negatively scored). The MOR score "describes the self from a moral-ethical perspective: examining moral worth, feeling of being a 'good' or 'bad' person" (Fitts and Warren 2003, p. 23). The moral self-concept score is related "to the sense of being able to control one's own impulses and behaviour" (Fitts and Warren 2003, p. 23). Table 5.6 presents the T-scores for Moral self-concept for the female and male students with intellectual disabilities.

Table 5.6 indicates that 60 % of the female students with intellectual disabilities and 80 % of the male students with intellectual disabilities obtained low MOR scores (below 40T). The remaining 40 % of the female students with intellectual disabilities and 20 % of the male students with intellectual disabilities scored MOR scores in the average range (above 40T and below 50T).

5.8 Personal Self-Concept

Items on the Personal Self-Concept (PER) scale include 'I'm happy with who I am' (positively scored) and 'I'm not important at all' (negatively scored). The PER score reflects "the individual's sense of personal worth, feeling of adequacy as a person and self evaluation of the personality apart from the body or relationships to others" (Fitts and Warren 2003, p. 23). The PER is a good reflection of overall personality integration, and particularly well adjusted individuals will obtain a high score on this dimension (Fitts and Warren 2003). Table 5.7 presents the T-scores for Personal self-concept for the female and male students with intellectual disabilities.

Table 5.7 Overview of T-scores for Personal self-concept

Female I.D. (N = 10)	Male I.D. (N = 10)
30	43
39	34
41	37
38	29
43	29
29	29
28	29
29	30
29	29
28	32

I.D. Students with intellectual disabilities

Table 5.7 indicates that 80 % of the female students with intellectual disabilities and 90 % of the male students with intellectual disabilities obtained low PER scores (less than or equal to 40T). The remaining 20 % of the female students with intellectual disabilities and 10 % of the male students with intellectual disabilities scored PER scores in the average range (above 40T and below 45T).

5.9 Family Self-Concept

The Family Self-Concept (FAM) scale includes such items as 'My family will always help me' (positively scored) and 'My family doesn't trust me' (negatively scored). The FAM score reflects "the individual's feelings of adequacy, worth and value as a family member. It refers to the individual's perception of self in relation to his/her immediate circle of associates" (Fitts and Warren 2003, p. 23). Table 5.8 presents the T-scores for Family self-concept for the female and male students with intellectual disabilities.

Table 5.8 indicates that 50 % of the female students with intellectual disabilities and 70 % of the male students with intellectual disabilities obtained low FAM scores (less than or equal to 40T). The remaining 50 % of the female students with intellectual disabilities and 30 % of the male students with intellectual disabilities scored FAM scores in the average range (above 40T and below 50T).

5.10 Social Self-Concept

The Social Self-Concept (SOC) scale includes such items as 'I get along well with other people' (positively scored) and 'I find it hard to talk with people I don't know' (negatively scored). The SOC dimension reflects in a more general way

Table 5.8 Overview of T-scores for Family self-concept

Female I.D. (N = 10)	Male I.D. (N = 10)
46	31
50	46
49	45
49	35
50	32
34	38
37	31
35	36
38	40
35	45

I.D. Students with intellectual disabilities

Table 5.9 Overview of T-scores for Social self-concept

Female I.D. (N = 10)	Male I.D. (N = 10)
41	30
47	38
46	41
41	31
44	30
32	32
35	32
38	33
35	35
32	36

I.D. Students with intellectual disabilities

"the individual's sense of adequacy and worth in social interaction with other people" (Fitts and Warren 2003, p. 24). Like the FAM score, the SOC score is a measure of how the self is perceived in relation to others. Table 5.9 presents the T-scores for Social self-concept for the female and male students with intellectual disabilities.

Table 5.9 indicates that 50 % of the female students with intellectual disabilities and 90 % of the male students with intellectual disabilities obtained low SOC scores (less than or equal to 40T). The remaining 50 % of the female students with intellectual disabilities and 10 % of the male students with intellectual disabilities scored SOC scores in the average range (above 40T and below 50T and 45T, respectively).

Table 5.10 Overview of T-scores for Academic self-concept

Female I.D. (N = 10)	Male I.D. (N = 10)
41	30
51	43
48	37
47	41
48	34
28	35
30	37
32	34
34	35
28	34

I.D. Students with intellectual disabilities

Table 5.11 Overview of T-scores for Total self-concept

Female I.D. (N = 10)	Male I.D. (N = 10)
37	28
44	37
44	38
40	29
43	24
25	26
27	25
28	28
28	29
27	33

I.D. Students with intellectual disabilities

5.11 Academic/Work Self-Concept

The Academic/Work Self-Concept (ACA) scale includes such items as 'Other people think I am smart' (positively scored) and 'I do not know how to work well' (negatively scored). The ACA score "is a measure of how people perceive themselves in school and work settings, and of how they believe they are seen by others in those settings" (Fitts and Warren 2003, p. 24). It is strongly related to actual academic performance (Fitts and Warren 2003). Table 5.10 presents the T-scores for Academic self-concept for the female and male students with intellectual disabilities.

Table 5.10 indicates that 50 % of the female students with intellectual disabilities and 80 % of the male students with intellectual disabilities obtained low ACA scores (less than or equal to 40T). The remaining 50 % of the female students with intellectual disabilities and 20 % of the male students with intellectual disabilities scored ACA scores in the average range (above 40T and below 55T and 45T, respectively).

5.12 Total Self-Concept

The Total Self-Concept (TOT) score is the single most important score on the TSCS: 2 (Fitts and Warren 2003). It reflects the individual's overall self concept and associated levels of self-esteem. It gives an indication of whether "an individual tends to hold a generally positive and consistent or negative and variable self-view" (Fitts and Warren 2003, p. 21). Table 5.11 presents the T-scores for Total self-concept for the female and male students with intellectual disabilities.

Table 5.11 indicates that 70 % of the female students with intellectual disabilities and 100 % of the male students with intellectual disabilities obtained low TOT scores (less than or equal to 40T). The remaining 30 % of the female students with intellectual disabilities scored TOT scores in the average range (above 40T and below 45T).

Reference

Fitts, W. H., & Warren, W. L. (2003). *Tennessee self-concept scale: Manual*. (2nd ed.). Los Angeles, CA: Western Psychological Services.

Chapter 6
Analysis of Stage 2 Interview Responses: Self-Concept

Abstract This chapter categorizes and analyses interview narratives into six prominent themes in relation to students with intellectual disabilities. It reports the views of students with intellectual disabilities, their parents' and their teachers' accounts of these students' physical, moral, personal, family, social and academic accomplishments. It identifies a number of reasons for the high or low self-concept of the students with intellectual disabilities. Students', parents' and teachers' views prove to be multidimensional and complex and hence add considerably to understanding how life and school experiences impact on the self-concept of the students concerned.

Keywords Physical self-concept · Moral self-concept · Personal self-concept · Family self-concept · Social self-concept · Academic self-concept

6.1 Introduction

The aim in interviewing participants in Stage 2 was to provide insights into the reasons for low or high self-concept in the students with intellectual disabilities under investigation. This chapter reports what students with intellectual disabilities were able to achieve in the different dimensions of self-concept. It further highlights the reasons for high or low self-concepts among these students.

In Stage 2, nine students with intellectual disabilities, four teachers and five parents were interviewed, totalling 18 interviews. The analytic process involved detailed reading of the interview narratives and coding the transcripts for the purpose of identifying common and dissimilar response patterns among them. The analysis followed the themes in the questions raised in the interviews. The themes identified for the analysis of Stage 2 interview data were Physical Self-Concept, Moral Self-Concept, Personal Self-Concept, Family Self-Concept, Social Self-Concept and Academic Self-Concept. The six themes were derived from the

P. Datta, *Students with Intellectual Disabilities*, SpringerBriefs in Education, DOI: 10.1007/978-981-287-017-9_6, © The Author(s) 2014

questionnaire in the analysis of the Stage 1 data. This chapter analyses the interview responses obtained under the themes.

Under each theme, questions similar in nature were asked of the three groups of participants-students with intellectual disabilities, their parents and teachers. As much as possible, selected quotations under each theme represent the spectrum of responses covered by all respondents in this study-students with intellectual disabilities, their parents and teachers. Some quotations are quite long, however. Rather than looking for meaning(s) in discrete words, the analysis concentrated on pools of information and overall meaning in order to remain as contextual and holistic as possible.

It must be reiterated that this research has not disclosed any information that could prejudice research participants, and for anonymity purposes, as stated in Chap. 4, each interviewee was given either a numeric or an alphabetic letter for identification purposes. This comprised the prefix ID (for students with intellectual disabilities) followed by a number (ID-1), T (for teachers) and P (for parents) followed by a letter from a to z (T-e, P-f). Teachers of students with ID are coded T-e to T-h. Parents of students with ID are coded P-f to P-j. In the sections that follow, the themes are discussed in turn, using illustrative quotations from the interviews as much as possible.

6.2 Physical Self-Concept

The discussion of the Physical self-concept theme presents the individuals' views of their state of health, explores whether they were able to practice a healthy way of life and what factors (if any) prevented them from achieving a healthy existence. To ensure this, a similar or comparable question was asked to the three groups of respondents-students with intellectual disabilities, their parents and teachers. The questions were as follows:

- The students:

"Do you maintain a physically healthy lifestyle? How do you achieve this? If not, why"?

- The parents:

"Does your child maintain a physically healthy lifestyle? If not, why"?

- The teachers:

"Do students with intellectual disabilities able to maintain a physically healthy lifestyle? If not, why"?

Table 6.1 summarizes the range of responses from the three groups of respondents.

Table 6.1 Overview of major response patterns from the interviews on Physical self-concept

Participants → Response patterns ↓	ID (N = 9)	Parents of ID (N = 5)	Teachers of ID (N = 4)
1. Maintaining/trying to maintain/expressed a desire to maintain a healthy lifestyle	ID-1, ID-2, ID-3, ID-4, ID-5, ID-11, ID-12, ID-13	P-f, P-g, P-h, P-i, P-j	
2. Disability a barrier to outdoor activities			T-g, T-h
3. Could maintain a fit routine only with help and support	ID-6	P-g, P-h, P-j	
4. Not maintaining a healthy state of living	ID-11		T-e, T-f, T-g, T-h
Total comments	10	8	6

ID Students with intellectual disabilities; *P* Parents; *T* Teachers

The major response patterns that emerged from the interviews with students, parents and teachers on Physical self-concept are discussed below.

6.2.1 Students with Intellectual Disabilities

Nine students with intellectual disabilities were asked about their lifestyle and how they maintained a healthy approach to life. All but two of the students with intellectual disabilities explained that they tried to maintain a healthy lifestyle by exercising, going for regular walks and eating a good and balanced diet. Some exhibited their desire of going beyond the regular regime by engaging in swimming and other activities as one student stated:

> I maintain a healthy lifestyle. I exercise regularly, eat healthy food. I go for jogs and run. On Thursday afternoon I run my dog and would like to go for Koala sports. (ID-1)
> I try to exercise and go for walks and I eat well. (ID-3)

There were a range of student sentiments that supported this sense of well being in a way that they related food and diet to a healthy lifestyle as the following quotes indicate:

> Partially, I maintain a healthy lifestyle because I take a healthy diet but I do not exercise. (ID-11)
> I try to keep fit by eating well and eating less fatty stuff. (ID-13)
> Hmm, I try to exercise, swim, and eat good food and diet. (ID-2)

Not all students reflected this level of confidence in their healthy lifestyle. For example, one of the students claimed that only with intervention from parents was it possible for her to maintain a healthy lifestyle. However, she emphasized that when she was left alone a feeling of dependency and negativism crept in.

Mum helps me to maintain a healthy lifestyle by feeding me with healthy diet and going out for long walks with me. Without mom's support, I feel alone and crave to depend on my mom (ID-6)

Therefore, in summary, it is evident that the majority of the students with intellectual disabilities seemed to be conscious and concerned about their physical health. To some their disability did not seem to prevent their keeping fit and maintaining a healthy lifestyle. This indicates that there is a definite desire and potential for this cohort of young people to develop a positive approach to physical fitness and healthy lifestyle; however to achieve this they require the intervention and assistance of significant others. Similarly, parents of intellectual disabilities predominantly reflected this positive disposition.

6.2.2 Parents of Students with Intellectual Disabilities

When parents were asked about their children's lifestyle, all five parents of students with intellectual disabilities confirmed that their children maintained or wanted to maintain a physically healthy lifestyle by going for walks, jogs and outdoor activities; although they reported that some of the students had to be constantly reminded or told to undertake those activities. For example, one parent reported:

She tries to keep fit by exercising and going for regular jogs. This has been imbibed in her from childhood for her betterment and general well being. (P-j)

Another commented:

I literally have to be after my daughter so that she can maintain a good lifestyle. She is not independent and in most instances needs to be reminded to go for jogs and swimming. (P-g)

Another parent expressed similar views:

My daughter seems to be pretty much concerned about her physical health. She tries going out for regular walks though sometimes she is lazy. (P-f)

Some parents recognized the centrality of sports in a healthy lifestyle and were concerned that their children did not always achieve this by themselves:

My son goes out for regular walks. He has the intention to engage in some sporty activities, however, he is too lazy to execute it himself. (P-i)

Another affirmed the role that teachers and schools played in achieving this healthy status:

I have seen my son trying to keep up to a good schedule. With help from teachers and parents he can fairly maintain a good lifestyle. (P-h)

None of the parents of the students with intellectual disabilities considered that their children were not maintaining a healthy lifestyle.

6.2.3 Teachers of Students with Intellectual Disabilities

When teachers were questioned about their perceptions of their students' physical lifestyle, all four teachers were of the opinion that their students with intellectual disabilities were often not able to maintain a physically healthy lifestyle. They reported that students with intellectual disabilities did not take part in any outdoor activities in school in the form of sports, clubs and teams. Further, they indicated that students were quite reluctant to engage in morning walks, jogs or exercise sessions. Some teachers attributed the student's inability to engage in healthy activities at school mainly to their intellectual disability. They claimed that students were not conscious of the importance of health, and to some extent were incapable of maintaining a regular healthy lifestyle for themselves. The teachers pointed out that student's required regular supervision and monitoring either by teachers or parents. Some of the teachers reflected this general sentiment as can be seen in the following excerpts:

> I think my students do not maintain a physically healthy lifestyle because most of them sat in front of the television at weekend and they do not get enough exercise and they don't play sports or join clubs and teams and that's a really big issue. I know my children spend all weekend on various sports and things they know at this age but these children don't. I know one student in the class who belongs to a team but no one else does anything. Most of them sit back at home and watch television. (T-e)
>
> No, most of them do not maintain a healthy lifestyle. They often spend time playing at the computer and never engage in outdoor sports in school. (T-f)
>
> I don't think so because they do not go for morning walks, in spite of me repeatedly telling them. I think it is because of their ID that they are not conscious and unable to meet the requirements of a physically fit lifestyle. (T-g)
>
> I would say, partially they are able to maintain a fit lifestyle because some parents I know are conscious and feed them with good and balanced diet. However, the students with ID are not able to do their parts by going for walks, runs or engaging in sports at school. They simply prefer to sit back and do indoor activities. (T-h)

6.2.4 Overview of Responses on Intellectual Disabilities

In summary, eight out of the nine students with intellectual disabilities articulated their intentions of maintaining a healthy way of life; one thought that she achieved it and another believed that only with help and intervention from significant others could she attain it. Parents of students with intellectual disabilities found that though their children had the urge to maintain healthy living, they had to be provided with help and assistance from teachers and parents to keep up to a healthy standard lifestyle. Teachers considered that their students with intellectual disabilities were incapable of maintaining a healthy daily life independently because of their disability and claimed they required systematic supervision and monitoring by parents and teachers. Therefore, it can be concluded that, in reference to the participants with intellectual disabilities, there were mixed perspectives regarding the physical self-concept of students in terms of their ability to achieve a healthy lifestyle. While the majority of the students self determined their status as healthy, parents held mixed views while teachers claimed the opposite. Whether these diverse views are evident in regards to students' moral self-concept, are explored in the next section.

6.3 Moral Self-Concept

The discussion of the Moral self-concept theme describes the self from an ethical and fair standpoint. It examines the moral worth, feelings of being and behaving the good and bad way. To ensure this a similar question was asked to the three groups of respondents-students with intellectual disabilities, their parents and teachers. The questions were as follows:

- The students:

    "Give examples (if any) of what you think is your good student behaviour and your bad student behaviour"?

- The parents:

    "Does your child engage in morally good or bad behaviour and why"?

- The teachers:

    "Do your students with intellectual disabilities demonstrate good or bad behaviour and why? What do you think could help students to improve their behaviour"?

    Table 6.2 summarizes the range of responses from the three groups of respondents.

6.3.1 Students with Intellectual Disabilities

When students were asked about their good and bad behaviours, four of the students with intellectual disabilities believed that they almost never exhibited any form of bad or immoral behaviour in class. They behaved well with friends and family, listened to teachers and preferred to be mostly quiet in class. The responses of these students have been summarized in the following excerpts:

> My good student behaviour is being nice to people and I did not indulge in any bad behaviour in my life. (ID-3)
>> I am kind to family and friends. I don't have any bad behaviour. (ID-2)
>> My good student behaviour is being always quiet. I have never been bad. (ID-5)

Table 6.2 Overview of major response patterns from the interviews on Moral self-concept

Participants → Response patterns ↓	ID (N = 9)	Parents of ID (N = 5)	Teachers of ID (N = 4)
1. Keen to listen to the teacher and displayed good behaviour	ID-2, ID-3, ID-5, ID-12	P-h, P-i	
2. Improper behaviour displayed by students occasionally (cause being antagonistic homes or cause not known)	ID-1, ID-6		
3. Mild impairment caused no behaviour problems; severe impairment caused disruptive behaviour in students			T-f
4. Negative behaviour exhibited by students due to their disability		P-f, P-h	T-e, T-f, T-g, T-h
5. Negative behaviour displayed by students due to mood swings		P-g, P-j	T-h
6. Negative behaviour displayed by students when no modifications were implemented by the teacher in the classroom			
7. Negative behaviour displayed by students when bullying occurred by non-disabled peers			T-h
8. No comment	ID-4, ID-11, ID-13		
Total comments	9	6	7

ID Students with intellectual disabilities; *P* Parents; *T* Teachers

One of the students with intellectual disabilities claimed that though she behaved well at school due to others watching her, she sometimes indulged in bad behaviour at home in the form of yelling and fighting with family members. She stated:

My bad student behaviour is only when I am back at home, I get angry and I yell. (ID-1)

It seemed that due to peer pressure she was somewhat compelled to behave well in class. However, once she reached home occasionally she vented her frustrations on family members. The findings also indicated that other students did not follow this pattern and continued their good behaviour from school to home.

6.3.2 Parents of Students with Intellectual Disabilities

When parents were asked about their children's moral behaviour, two of the parents reported that their children were honest, obedient, helpful and trustworthy. However, all four of the parents confirmed that sometimes their children with intellectual disabilities exhibited temper tantrums, stubborn and aggressive behaviour at home mainly due to depression or mood swings which they believed was due to their children's mild intellectual disabilities. These were the times when the children were not in absolute control of their behaviour and it would not be fair to judge their moral behaviour based on such situations. According to parents, schools, teachers and counsellors should teach students with intellectual disabilities coping strategies to deal effectively with their behaviour during these times. Selective views of parents on these sentiments are represented below:

> I feel my child always is keen to display good behaviour and tries to be honest, kind and helpful with people around him. (P-i)
> Generally, yes. But sometimes she can be quite difficult and obstinate to handle, fails to understand obvious things and it is partly because of her ID. (P-f)
> Hmm, I would say fairly not so much at home. I am not sure about her moral behaviour at school but at home she sometimes engages in temper tantrums. I feel she is not able to exercise the right kind of control over her behaviour, mainly due to her mood swings which she is not aware of. (P-g)
> I feel my son is obedient and otherwise quite honest. Well, sometimes he can be disruptive, rude and insensitive though not intentional. This I feel is because of his mild ID. (P-h)
> Yes, generally my daughter is good to people though sometimes she sets in depression and those are the times when she exhibits not so polite and decent kind of behaviour. But those are the times when she does not feel good and she is not in control of herself. (P-j)

6.3.3 Teachers of Students with Intellectual Disabilities

When teachers were asked about the moral behaviour of their students, all four teachers were of the opinion that students with intellectual disabilities sometimes displayed inappropriate behaviour in class. However, the exhibition of such negative behaviours should not be misconstrued that students were immoral. Most of their behaviour were unintentional and due to their disability. The following quotes represent the opinions of teachers:

> I feel students with ID sometimes are not able to control their emotions adequately and an outburst of it is often displayed in the classroom. (T-g)
> With our students, a lot of them its disability and not intentional—it's just as a result of their disability. (T-e)

One of the teachers confirmed that students' behaviour depended a lot on the degree and severity of their impairment. If a child was diagnosed to have a mild and borderline case of intellectual impairment, then his behaviour can be taught to be controlled, desirable and courteous by teachers. She said:

> Well, some students with ID are not able to engage in good and appropriate behaviour in class mainly due to their ID. Sometimes, it depends on the degree of impairment. If it is a mild and fairly borderline case, the child with ID can be taught to behave well in class. (T-f)

Another teacher believed that much depended on the behaviour demonstrated by other peers in class towards students with intellectual disabilities. She claimed that if peers were considerate and helpful towards students with intellectual disabilities and included them in all activities during and after school hours, students with intellectual disabilities were found to exhibit positive and constructive behaviour in class. She commented:

> Some students with ID are not able to exhibit good moral behaviour in class. But that does not mean that they are immoral in their daily lives. Their disruptive behaviour is most of the times due to mood swings and their ID and during these they are most often not aware of how they behave. Sometimes, their behaviour (whether positively or negatively) depends a lot on the ability of their peers to show proper and positive behaviour towards them. (T-h)

6.3.4 Overview of Responses on Intellectual Disabilities

In summary, most of the students with intellectual disabilities and their parents agreed that usually students were quite well behaved in class and tried to show positive behaviour towards others except in rare circumstances due to factors beyond their control, they demonstrated some disruptive and disorderly behaviour at home. Therefore, parents were of the opinion that it would not be fair and just to judge the moral behaviour of their children with intellectual disabilities based on those situations. Teachers also expressed their views on similar lines and asserted that the inappropriate and unruly behaviour sometimes exhibited by students with intellectual disabilities were unintentional and caused due to factors over which they have little control. Whether views similar in pattern are apparent in regards to personal self-concept, are explored in the next section.

6.4 Personal Self-Concept

The discussion of the Personal self-concept theme reflects the individuals' sense of personal value, merit and traits, feelings of capability as a person, able to solve problems independently and confidently and self-evaluation of one's personality. This dimension reflects the overall personality integration of one-self. To investigate the personal self-concept of the students, the following two interview questions similar in nature were asked to the three groups of respondents-students with intellectual disabilities, their parents and teachers. The questions were as follows:

• The students:

"Tell me about yourself. How would you describe what kind of a person you are"?
and

"When you are having a problem, how do you go about solving it? Do you find problems difficult"?

- The parents:

  "What kind of a person is your child and why"?
  and
  "How does your child go about solving problems? How can your child be helped to solve problems in a better way"?

- The teachers:

  "Describe your students with intellectual disabilities"?
  and
  "How do your students with intellectual disabilities go about solving problems? What could help them to solve problems in a better way"?

  Table 6.3 summarizes the range of responses from the three groups of respondents.

6.4.1 Students with Intellectual Disabilities

When students with intellectual disabilities were interviewed to describe themselves, eight out of nine students considered themselves to be nice, friendly, kind, trustworthy and responsible. The responses of two students, listed below indicated that they were generally liked by their peers and others because they were honest, helpful and obliging in nature:

> I am trustworthy, smart and always happy and bubbling. I have lot of friends. (ID-13)
>   I am a responsible, kind, wonderful person and I reckon the people whom I meet like to get close to me. I go to the mainstream and have lots of friends there. (ID-1)

When students with intellectual disabilities were asked how they solved their problems, seven of them confirmed that it was impossible for them to solve problems independently. Much was also contingent on the magnitude of the problem as well. But usually, the majority of them found problems quite overwhelming and difficult. They often sought the help of peers, teachers or sometimes elders as demonstrated in the quotes below:

> I can't solve problems myself. I have to consult friends and parents. (ID-4)
>   I tell my problems mainly to my teachers. (ID-5)
>   I can't solve problems myself. (ID-6)
>   I prefer to work out my problems by talking to friends, teachers and families. (ID-13)

Overall, a few students expressed an urge to be more independent and to solve problems themselves. But often due to their intellectual disability, they lacked judicious strategies and effective coping mechanisms to combat real life problems, requiring the intervention of others.

Table 6.3 Overview of major response patterns from the interviews on Personal self-concept

Participants → Response patterns ↓	ID (N = 9)	Parents of ID (N = 5)	Teachers of ID (N = 4)
1. Students were found to have positive traits	ID-1, ID-2, ID-3, ID-4, ID-5, ID-11, ID-12, ID-13	P-f, P-j	T-f, T-h
2. Students were uncommunicative, restrained and felt low due to their disability		P-g, P-i	T-g
3. Students were found to be reactive and sensitive towards others opinion		P-f, P-g, P-h, P-j	T-g, T-h
4. Students never ventured any new/ challenging enterprise		P-g	
5. Students had to depend on others for their problems/ crucial tasks	ID-2, ID-3, ID-4, ID-5, ID-6, ID-12, ID-13	P-f, P-g, P-h, P-i, P-j	T-e, T-f, T-g, T-h
Total comments	15	14	9

ID Students with intellectual disabilities; *P* Parents; *T* Teachers

6.4.2 Parents of Students with Intellectual Disabilities

When parents were asked what kind of a person their child was, two of the parents believed that their children were reliable, responsible and helpful in most situations:

> Well, I feel my daughter can be quite helpful and reliable in certain instances. (P-f)
> My daughter is a friendly, cheerful nice girl. (P-j)

Another two of the parents noted their children with intellectual disabilities to be shy and secluded from their peers, mainly because they were labelled and branded by their peers:

> He is quiet, shy and sometimes prefers to be secluded and lonely. I think he is not comfortable and at ease in his peer group, owing mainly due to his intellectual impairment. Sometimes, his peers make fun of him and label him to be foolish and silly which really upsets him. (P-i)

Four of the parents found their children to be sensitive and reactive at times to the opinion of peers. This often led to depression and frustration among these students as is evident from the quotes below:

> However, she can be quite reactive and argumentative to people whom she doesn't' like. (P-f)
> My child is quite sensitive and reactive to others, especially if anyone bullies her due to her ID. (P-g)
> What I have observed of him is that he is better off at home rather than school. At school, I feel some negative behaviour from his peers (due to his ID) triggers him off and can be the cause of displaying any rude behaviour from his end. His teachers, I feel should be more cautious about this. (P-h)

> Though I have seen her behaving well with people on most occasions she may engage
> sometimes in aggressive and rude behaviour when she is not feeling that well. (P-j)

In terms of solving problems, all five parents reported that their children with intellectual disabilities often resorted to help and assistance from teachers, parents and the school Counsellor. While parents appreciated and encouraged the help taken from teachers and school Counsellors, they did not welcome the idea of seeking advice from peers as parents believed that children with intellectual disabilities might end up receiving the wrong information from peers. Three of the parents further attested that they could not depend and rely much on the peers of their children with intellectual disabilities, as peers often were the main source of bully and discontentment in their children's lives. These views of parents are evident in the quotes below:

> She often needs help from me to solve her problems. Schools should help her to be more
> independent to solve her problems. (P-f)
>   Hmm, that's a difficult one. Okay, I would say in all possibilities my child needs
> assistance to solve her problems. I feel the school Counsellor should play a positive role in
> this regard. The school Counsellor should help her by providing her strategies to get her
> problems solved. (P-g)
>   My daughter often resorts to her friends for quick solution. I feel she should be getting
> the right kind of advice from her teachers and the school Counsellor. (P-j)
>   My child needs help and support from others to solve his problems. Though I have seen
> the urge in him as not to depend on others. But sometimes due to the nature of his
> problems (can be quite serious) he needs help from outside. What I fear is that he may be
> receiving the wrong kind of advice from his friends. So I would not encourage him to
> depend too much on friends. (P-h)

Generally, students with intellectual disabilities were found to rely too much on others in solving their problems which could later have an adverse effect on their independent problem solving skills.

6.4.3 Teachers of Students with Intellectual Disabilities

When teachers were asked to describe their students with intellectual disabilities, one of them commented that she found her students to be shy, introvert and aloof from most of their peers in class. According to the teacher, some of her students with intellectual disabilities participated in a small and known group. They feared to interact with new people, lest they became the subject of bullying:

> Some I have noticed to be shy and introvert as they prefer to remain aloof and are unable
> to mingle with the class. But this could be because of their ID and also because they could
> be bullied. (T-g)

Two of the teachers found their students exhibited rude, aggressive and hostile behaviour in class but those were the times purely attributed to mood swings and depressions which these students encountered from time to time. This is evident in the quote below:

I would say some of them can be hostile, aggressive and disruptive but again that is because of their impairment and mood swings. (T-g)

One of the teachers, further commented that sometimes, new teachers were not adequately trained and inexperienced to handle students with intellectual disabilities and that could cast a negative impact on the behaviour of these students. The response below confirms the claim made by the teacher:

Some teachers are not trained enough to handle students with ID and that is when the problem comes in. In such situations, the teacher can't handle the student with ID and the student in turn engages in hostile and insensitive behaviour in class. But this is occasional and may not always be the case. (T-h)

On a positive note, according to two teachers, students with mild intellectual disabilities were able to display positive traits; however, they needed teachers and parents to play an active role to facilitate the desirable behaviour in them:

Students with ID can be responsible, understanding only with extra and caring effort from teachers. (T-h)

When teachers were asked as to how students with intellectual disabilities go about solving their problems, all four teachers confirmed that these students did not possess the necessary skills and expertise to solve their own problems. They constantly required the help of teachers and parents from time to time. Two of the teachers devised good strategies for students with intellectual disabilities to help them solve their own problems. These teachers provided students with real life case examples and problems, set up different problem scenarios and then prompted them with strategies to deal and manage those problem areas. This is a clear indication that teachers are striving to prepare their students with intellectual disabilities for the larger real world, outside the boundaries of the school as is evident in the quotes below:

Students with ID can never solve their problems on their own. They need considerable help and attention from teachers and parents. (T-f)

I feel that students with ID just cannot solve problems on their own. Left alone, they might be lost and completely swayed away. Teachers and parents have to constantly be on the go to find out about their problems and devise strategies for them to solve them. (T-g)

Students with ID need the help and assistance from others to solve their problems. They do not have the skills and expertise to get things sorted out on its own. Providing them with real life case examples is a good way to teach them to handle problems. (T-h)

We, in class, we do examples and we probe play and we set up different scenarios like, say what would you do in this situation and I think for some of them like it a bit but others doesn't help. (T-e)

6.4.4 Overview of Responses on Intellectual Disabilities

In summary, eight of the students with intellectual disabilities described themselves as possessing many optimistic and constructive qualities. Parents, however, pointed out that their children were often labelled by other non-disabled peers to be foolish which was the cause of many introverted and depressive symptoms habitually occurring within students with intellectual disabilities. Teachers noted negative and aggressive behaviour in students with intellectual disabilities; however, they attributed the causes to be bullying, students' cognitive deficits, mood swings and inexperienced teachers. The interview responses from all the three groups of participants-students, their parents and teachers established that students with intellectual disabilities did not possess the necessary skills and expertise to solve their problems independently and in almost every situation necessitated the help and assistance from close acquaintances. The family lives of the students are investigated in the next section.

6.5 Family Self-Concept

The discussion of the Family self-concept theme reflects the individual student participants' feelings of satisfaction, importance and merit as a family member and their perceptions about their family. It refers to the individual's relationship to their immediate relatives in the form of parents and siblings. To determine this, a similar question was asked to the three groups of respondents-students with intellectual disabilities, their parents and teachers. The questions were as follows:

• The students:

    "Tell me about your family? What kind of relationship do you share with your family members"?

• The parents:

    "What kind of relationship do you and other members in your family have with your child and why"?

• The teachers:

    "What is the relationship between your students with intellectual disabilities and their family members and why"?
    Table 6.4 summarizes the range of responses from the three groups of respondents.

6.5.1 Students with Intellectual Disabilities

When students with intellectual disabilities were asked about their family lives, eight of the students with intellectual disabilities claimed to share happy, contented and satisfied family relationships. These students reported they got along well with

Table 6.4 Overview of major response patterns from the interviews on Family self-concept

Participants → Response patterns ↓	ID (N = 9)	Parents of ID (N = 5)	Teachers of ID (N = 4)
1. Students share a good and amiable family relationship with some members	ID-2, ID-3, ID-4, ID-5, ID-6, ID-11, ID-12, ID-13	P-g	T-e
2. Students share a distant relation with a non-disabled sibling only		P-h	
3. Students share a detached relation with their biological parents			
4. Students share an unfriendly relation with their family members due to their disability or if they have a step/ single parent		P-h, P-i, P-j	T-h
5. Students are found to share a considerate relation with another sibling with disability	ID-1	P-g	T-f
6. Female students/mothers are found to share a better relation as compared to their male counterparts/ fathers		P-f	T-g
Total comments	9	7	4

ID Students with intellectual disabilities; *P* Parents; *T* Teachers

other siblings, parents and sometimes with grandparents as well. Students with intellectual disabilities commented:

> I share a good relationship with my family. Mum works till 5 p.m. We go out on the weekends. I have three sisters and one brother and we share good relationships. (ID-2)
>
> My family (mum+ dad+ nanny+ brothers+ sisters), all are nice. (ID-3)
>
> My mum has been divorced long time ago. My mum is single and I stay with my mum. I have my brother. I share a good relationship with my mum and brother. (ID-5)
>
> My family constitutes of my grandpa, grandma and my sisters. We all share a good relationship. My sister lives somewhere else and I just live with my grandma and grandpa. (ID-13)
>
> I live with my mum. I see my dad every second weekend. I get along well with my three sisters. (ID-6)

One of the students with intellectual disabilities seemed to get along well with her sibling also with a disability. This is evident from her quote below:

> I live with my other sister because she has a disability and I understand her well. We all love each other and we do fun stuff. (ID-1)

6.5.2 Parents of Students with Intellectual Disabilities

When parents were asked about their children's family lives, one of the parents commented that her daughter with intellectual disabilities was able to share a good and pleasant relationship with family members. According to this parent, family relationships were good and agreeable for her child with intellectual disability because there was another sibling with disability too in the family:

> Well, my husband and I share a comfortable and understanding relationship with my daughter. My elder daughter is disabled too and she can understand the younger one quite well. They get along well and we seem to be a happy family. (P-g)

However, three other parents commented that in families where there were step parents or non-disabled siblings, often conflicts and discord arose with the child with intellectual disability. It was in such situations where the child with intellectual disability believed that they were not cared for and loved in the family. Such diverse views of parents are represented in the quotes below:

> I try my level best to understand my son well. There are times when he can become quite hostile and insensitive towards his other siblings and that are when the conflict sets in. (P-h)
>
>   Sometimes, I have found my son too inert and withdrawn that he does not share his problems with me. It could be due to a mistrust developed in him due to his step father. He feels that his step father doesn't love him and he doesn't feel comfortable sharing his problems with me (P-i)

One of the parents interestingly commented that a female child with intellectual disability seemed to share a better and friendlier relationship with family members when compared to a male child with intellectual disability. She even went on to comment that it was always easier to handle a daughter rather than a son with intellectual disabilities:

> I share a good and contented relationship with my daughter. I feel since I am blessed with a girl child, it is always easier to handle and understand a girl child compared to a boy child. (P-f)

6.5.3 Teachers of Students with Intellectual Disabilities

When teachers were asked about the family lives of their students with intellectual disabilities, a common trend observed by one of the teachers was that usually students with intellectual disabilities had a good family life if they had another sibling with disability. In such situations, the siblings were known to understand each other's problems and situation well. One teacher reported:

> Usually, students with ID have a good relationship if they have another sibling with disability as well. In such situations, both siblings understand each other well. (T-f)

Another teacher noted that mothers were found to share a close and more intimate relationship with their child with intellectual disability as compared to fathers. The reason cited by the teacher was that mothers were more patient, considerate and understanding, typical of motherly traits in comparison to fathers, especially when dealing with a child with impairment. The teacher said:

> I will say that my students with ID share a good relationship with their mothers because I feel mothers can be more patient, considerate and understanding towards them compared to their fathers or other siblings. (T-g)

Two other teachers also found that students with intellectual disabilities were well adjusted to their family life if they did not have a step parent as often these students felt that they were not cared for or wanted in the family by the step parents. Students with intellectual disabilities anticipated that their step parent perceived them to be a burden in the family and this strained relationships amongst family members. This is evident in the following quotes:

> Students with ID usually share a healthy relationship and are close with family members. One student I remember had a very hostile home environment because his mother was divorced and he felt that his step father simply hated him and didn't bother for his well being at all. (T-h)
> I had a student last year that didn't get any help from step parent. (T-e)

6.5.4 Overview of Responses on Intellectual Disabilities

In summary, eight of the students with intellectual disabilities generally shared good and amiable family relationships, preferably with a sibling with disability. Parents and teachers were also of the view that students with intellectual disabilities were found to share a pleasant relationship with another sibling with disability. However, family discontent arose in situations where a non-disabled sibling or a step-parent seemed to be insensitive to the requirements of the child with intellectual disabilities. One of the parents believed that it was easier to handle a girl child with intellectual disabilities in comparison to a boy child with intellectual disabilities. One of the teachers recognized that mothers were more intimate, thoughtful and considerate towards a child with impairment in comparison to fathers. Whether such divergent responses emerged in regards to social self-concept, are explored in the next section.

6.6 Social Self-Concept

The discussion of the Social self-concept theme reflects how the self is perceived in relation to others. It refers in a more general way to the individual's ability to interact socially with others, especially with peers. To explore students', parents' and teachers' views of the way the students with intellectual disdabilities under investigation interact with friends, they were asked the following questions:

- The students:

  "Who do you like to mix with and why? What would help you to interact better with friends"?

- The parents:

"How is your child's social life and why? What do you think would help your child to interact better with friends"?

- The teachers:

"Describe your students with intellectual disabilities' social life with peers? What could help students in their social interaction"?

Table 6.5 summarizes the range of responses from the three groups of respondents.

6.6.1 Students with Intellectual Disabilities

When students with intellectual disabilities were asked about their social lives, four out of nine students commented on their social behaviour and stated that they were usually quiet and reticent and were unable to interact well on most occasions. These four typically described themselves to be introverted. One of them even preferred to listen to music during lunch hours rather than interacting with peers. One of these four students, on a positive note, expressed a keen desire to interact with more and more friends. These views of students with intellectual disabilities are confirmed by the following quotes:

> I don't like to mix with people. I could interact better. (ID-2)
> I am not friendly and people don't talk to me much. (ID-4)
> I interact not so well. (ID-12)
> I do not have a proper social life due to my disability in school. I put my music on my ears during lunch and recess time. (ID-6)

Five other students claimed that they had many friends and always wanted to interact with everyone in school. However, in a group situation one of the students resorted more to listening to their peers as opposed to conversing with them. The following quote substantiates this:

> I like to mix with everyone in school. I can interact better by listening to friends more, not interrupting them while they are talking. (ID-1)

Two out of the five students believed that sometimes they experienced some difficulties in initiating a new conversation or sustaining any discussion in a group situation:

> I like to mix with everybody in school. Sometimes, I find it difficult to start a conversation. (ID-13)
> Yes, I like to talk to friends. I go to the mainstream and have friends. I find it hard at times to carry conversations in a group situation. (ID-11)

Table 6.5 Overview of major response patterns from the interviews on Social self-concept

Participants → Response patterns ↓	ID (N = 9)	Parents of ID (N = 5)	Teachers of ID (N = 4)
1. Students interacted well with peers especially who had common interests to share	ID-1, ID-3, ID-5, ID-11, ID-13		T-e, T-g, T-h
2. Students unable to interact well due to their disability	ID-6	P-f, P-g, P-h, P-i, P-j	T-e, T-g, T-h
3. Students did not interact with friends by choice or due to their family being isolated	ID-2, ID-4, ID-12		
4. Students unable to interact well due to not owning their own transport			
5. Students noted to have many online friends; however, not in the real classroom			T-f
Total comments	9	5	4

ID Students with intellectual disabilities; *P* Parents; *T* Teachers

Another student indicated that he could interact better with mainstream peers only if they were in a problem situation and by helping them; he could fit well into the group:

> I mix with the mainstream kids. I could interact better by sticking up with my friends if they have trouble and by helping them. (ID-5)

6.6.2 Parents of Students with Intellectual Disabilities

When parents were asked about their children's social lives, they tended to focus on their children's social behaviour and in doing so, five of the parents described their children with intellectual disabilities as shy, reclusive and lonely. Two of the parents noted that though their children with intellectual disabilities had the enthusiasm and interest to meet new people, their intellectual impairment often came in the way of their interaction. Parents indicated that what these students feared was they might be the subject of mockery and sarcasm in public which they had often experienced in the classroom in the presence of their peers. They explained that repetition of this negative experience a number of times led students to believe that they were not as worthy and intelligent as their peers, which in turn caused them to isolate themselves. Some of the interview responses which confirm this are as follows:

> My daughter is quite shy and introvert. She does not have many friends. Teachers, I think should play an active part in breaking the ice between her and her friends. (P-f)

I think my daughter's social life is quite boring. She is often left out when her friends are into some parties. Schools should do something about this. They should be involving her more in group discussions and pairing activities. (P-g)

I would say his social life is awkward. He is shy and embarrassed to interact with new people. Sometimes, he had to experience some bullying from his friends because of his ID which has left him more shy and depressed. (P-h)

I would say that generally he is quite eager to meet and interact with new people. But there is something that stops him. Probably his impairment comes in action. Teachers, school Counsellors should be looking into this and build their communication and social abilities in a more positive manner. (P-i)

I have seen the enthusiasm in my daughter to interact, talk and share things with her friends. However, there is something that does not allow her to mix freely with people. Probably her intellectual impairment does not allow her to interact wholeheartedly with her friends, lest she should become the object of ridicule at school. (P-j)

Therefore, the evidence from the parents' interviews clearly shows that students with intellectual disabilities tended to have a boring, isolated and awkward social life and most parents believed that teachers should intervene in such situations.

6.6.3 Teachers of Students with Intellectual Disabilities

When teachers were asked about the social lives of their students with intellectual disabilities, all four teachers found that students with intellectual disabilities preferred to stay secluded and isolated in the mainstream classes and lacked proper social networks with their non-disabled peers. One of the teachers established that students with intellectual disabilities had greater friends online as compared to the mainstream classrooms. A possible reason cited by her, was that these students were receiving greater comfort and warmth from their online friends as opposed to their mainstream classroom peers. It seemed that the non-disabled peers were simply not bothered to include students with intellectual disabilities in their social hang-outs and private parties. The following excerpts from the teacher interviews confirm this:

Non-disabled peers do not invite students with ID for social gatherings and parties which is a main reason for this social gap. (T-g)

They might fear that their disability might not be welcomed by everyone and they simply cannot get along well with new people. (T-h)

This really depends on the students individual characteristics. Some can interact well while some don't. I have seen that some students with ID have more number of friends online as compared to the school. (T-f)

Three of the teachers also noted that students with intellectual disabilities interacted well and had many friends if they were attending a special setting as compared to a mainstream class. In a special setting they could connect well with other students with disabilities because they had common interests to share with one another and understood each other well. This was acknowledged in the following excerpts:

I have seen that the general trend is students with ID can interact with peers who have a disability as well, somehow they seem not to get along peers who are non-disabled. (T-g)

In the special school setting, its I would say it's in their disabilities, it is a very close knit group and the class is very supportive and there is no bullying, no teasing, nothing like that and most of them can get on very well with each other. (T-e)

What I have seen that students with ID can interact well with peers if they are in a special setting with only children with disabilities. However, in mainstream setting students with ID do not have that social bond with non-disabled students. (T-h)

6.6.4 Overview of Responses on Intellectual Disabilities

In summary, four of the students with intellectual disabilities did not interact well with peers and even the ones who believed that they could interact well, faced difficulties in initiating or sustaining a conversation with peers. These students mostly remained restrained, uncommunicative and isolated. All parents and teachers found students with intellectual disabilities to be isolated and secluded from their mainstream peers. Some parents believed that these students were the object of scorn and contempt by students without disabilities due to their cognitive impairments. Three of the teachers found students with intellectual disabilities to interact well only with peers with disabilities in a special setting. Students with intellectual disabilities were noted by one of the teachers to have great social networks online, however, not so in their regular classrooms. Whether such unique responses are found in regards to the academic self-concept, are explored in the next section.

6.7 Academic Self-Concept

The discussion of the Academic self-concept theme refers to how students perceive themselves in school and college settings and how spontaneously and easily they can approach new tasks and learning. The academic self-concept focused on students' learning and did not compartmentalize itself into different school subjects. The three groups of respondents-students with intellectual disabilities, their parents and teachers were asked the following:

- The students:

"How do you go about learning new things"?

- The parents:

"How does your child go about learning new things and why? What could help him/her in this respect"?

- The teachers:

"How do your students with intellectual disabilities go about learning new things? What could help them in this respect"?

Table 6.6 summarizes the range of responses from the three groups of respondents.

6.7.1 Students with Intellectual Disabilities

When students with intellectual disabilities were questioned as to how they go about learning new things, one of the students claimed that she generally took more time to learn new things as compared to her non-disabled peers:

> I can't learn new things quickly in comparison to my friends. (ID-4)

However, seven of the students with intellectual disabilities expressed a keen desire and eagerness for new learning. Sometimes, they could learn things easily, depending on the level of difficulty of the new learning. Most students devised their own strategies to learn new tasks. Some believed that practise makes perfect and by repetition/ working on a task again and again they could master it well. Others learned from modelling or maintaining a routine to learn new things. One of the students expressed her concerns in any learning related to Mathematics, English and sometimes Australian Studies. These discrete views of the students with intellectual disabilities are demonstrated in the ensuing quotes:

> I can learn new things by playing/ practising new games which helps my memory. (ID-2)
> I learn new things by working over it again and again. (ID-3)
> I can learn new things through modelling and repetition. (ID-6)
> In some ways I am a quick learner. I have a routine of learning new things. However, I have difficulty learning in Mathematics, sometimes in English and a bit in Australian Studies. (ID-1)

Therefore, the interview responses indicated that students with intellectual disabilities often possessed the zeal and impetus to learn new things and devised their own techniques to accomplish new learning, a positive dimension.

6.7.2 Parents of Students with Intellectual Disabilities

When parents were asked how their children go about learning new things, three of the parents described their children with intellectual disabilities as slow and time consuming learners:

> I feel my daughter is generally slow in learning new things compared to her peers. She needs more repetition and practice. (P-f)

Table 6.6 Overview of major response patterns from the interviews on Academic self-concept

Participants → Response patterns ↓	ID (N = 9)	Parents of ID (N = 5)	Teachers of ID (N = 4)
1. Students exhibited a readiness and willingness for new learning	ID-1, ID-2, ID-3, ID-5, ID-6, ID-12, ID-13	P-g, P-j	
2. Students found it difficult and time consuming for new learning mainly due to their disability	ID-4	P-f, P-h, P-i	T-f, T-h
3. Students interpreted failure easily and quickly for new learning		P-g	
4. Students new learning depends on any 3 factors: teacher's skills and efforts, provision of proper resources and family support			T-e, T-g, T-h
5. No comment	ID-11		
Total comments	9	6	5

ID Students with intellectual disabilities; *P* Parents; *T* Teachers

> My son is slow in learning new things because of his ID. But he has to be helped to learn in his own way. He is very impatient and fidgety with new learning. (P-h)
> I wouldn't rate my son as a competent learner. He has poor concentration. He needs more assistance, practice and help to master new skills. (P-i)

Two other parents claimed that their children with intellectual disabilities demonstrated the desire and urge for new learning; however, one out of the two argued that her daughter interpreted failure too often and too quickly which discouraged her from engaging in new learning:

> My daughter has the zeal and enthusiasm to learn new things. It is only with abstract concepts that she finds it difficult to understand. (P-j)
> My daughter has got the urge in her to learn and grasp new concepts. However, she interprets that she would meet failure too often and gives up the task at hand too easily. She is often easily distracted. Teachers should be more consistent and have more patience in dealing with her. They should spend more time on her, on a one on one basis. (P-g)

The general trend that emerged from parents' interview responses were that students with intellectual disabilities lacked concentration skills, were restless and gave up the task in hand too quickly. Parents believed that more support, assistance and cooperation from schools and teachers in the learning of students with intellectual disabilities are needed.

6.7.3 Teachers of Students with Intellectual Disabilities

When teachers were asked as to how their students go about learning new things, two out of four teachers noted students with intellectual disabilities fall behind in the academic arena mainly because of their intellectual deficiencies. According to these teachers, students with intellectual disabilities took more time and required extra effort to learn and grasp new concepts. These students generally took longer compared to their non-disabled peers to understand new learning and needed constant supervision by teachers in their learning processes. Three of the teachers believed that students with intellectual disabilities benefitted greatly from one on one interactions, the inclusion of hands on activities, constant drilling and repetition of the same activities again and again. Some of the subsequent quotes represent this:

> Students with ID are not able to learn new things quickly mainly because of their intellectual deficiencies as they take more time in understanding things compared to their peers. (T-f)
> Students with ID generally take more time and require extra effort to learn new things and this could make their whole learning journey frustrating and boring as well. More one on one dealings and hand on activities can make new learning comparatively easier for them. (T-h)
> More one on one, that's what affects me, more one o' one. We have one exercise for 11 students and most of our students, not all of our students' need one on one—and that would help. (T-e)
> I feel some students with mild ID can learn new things with regular drilling and more effort on the part of the teachers. By making students practice and repeat a task again and again, students with ID do learn new information. (T-g)

6.7.4 Overview of Responses on Intellectual Disabilities

In summary, although seven of the students with intellectual disabilities demonstrated an ardent desire for new learning, one of the students revealed that he could not learn new things as easily and spontaneously as his non-disabled peers, owing mainly to his intellectual disability. Overall the findings from the interviews revealed that students with intellectual disabilities required a greater amount of drilling, practice, repetition and modelling. Parents too confirmed that their children with intellectual disabilities lacked concentration skills due to their cognitive deficits and interpreted failures too often and early which were some of the reasons for them to grasp new concepts slowly. Teachers were also of the opinion that students with intellectual disabilities took more time, required extra help and needed constant monitoring and supervision to learn and perform new activities.

Chapter 7
Discussion

Abstract This chapter discusses and interprets the survey questionnaire and interview findings along the six dimensions of self-concept, Physical, Moral, Personal, Family, Social and Academic Self-Concepts and thus, Total Self-Concept for all students with intellectual disabilities. These findings are supported and contrasted with the literature, wherever available. There has been a dearth of studies in the past investigating the self-concept along the six dimensions in students with intellectual disabilities and therefore, literature similar to this study is difficult to locate. In this chapter, self-concept is used as a key variable to unlock understanding of the many social, family, personal, emotional and educational problems that students with intellectual disabilities have experienced in this study.

Keywords Physical self-concept · Moral self-concept · Personal self-concept · Family self-concept · Social self-concept · Academic self-concept

7.1 Introduction

This chapter discusses the significant and key findings obtained under the themes (identified in Chaps. 5 and 6) for students with intellectual disabilities. The findings have been supported by or contrasted with previous studies wherever possible. The main derivations and interpretations of the key themes identified in relation to self-concept for students with intellectual disabilities are discussed in the following main sections.

7.2 Self-Concept of Students with Intellectual Disabilities

This section contains the noteworthy findings that emerged from the questionnaire and interview responses along the different dimensions of self-concept for students with intellectual disabilities. It should be noted that no previous studies have

P. Datta, *Students with Intellectual Disabilities*, SpringerBriefs in Education, DOI: 10.1007/978-981-287-017-9_7, © The Author(s) 2014

investigated exclusively the various dimensions of self-concept only for students with intellectual disabilities in the way that this study has.

7.2.1 Physical Self-Concept

The great majority of the students with intellectual disabilities obtained low scores in physical self-concept. The interview responses confirmed that the majority of the students with intellectual disabilities made an effort to stay healthy, go for regular walks and also engage in outdoor activities. However, for a very few students their disability was such that they could not keep up their physical health independently; they had to rely on others and this dependence was a deterrent to maintaining the right and ideal kind of lifestyle. Parents expressed similar sentiments to students. This positive effort initiated by students with intellectual disabilities can be nurtured, developed and channelled by parents and teachers to assist them in narrowing the gap between their scores obtained and their efforts pursued on this dimension.

According to teachers, students with intellectual disabilities were not health conscious and found it difficult to recognize the adverse long term negative effects that a poor lifestyle could cast on their health. Thus, because most of these students had little opportunity to develop intrinsic motivation for maintaining healthy life styles, they became lazy, sat back at home and watched television. In such situations, the home and the school should play equal roles to provide some extrinsic motivation for students with intellectual disabilities so that they are able to keep up to the minimum standards of maintaining a healthy lifestyle.

7.2.2 Moral Self-Concept

The majority of the students with intellectual disabilities had low scores in moral self-concept. The remaining students with intellectual disabilities (slightly more than a quarter) obtained moral self-concept scores in the normal range.

The interview responses conveyed that sometimes, students with intellectual disabilities displayed obedience, compliance and introvert traits. However, there were other times when they were found to engage in aggressive and obstinate behaviour, more often in home than school. Parents and teachers commented that the negative behaviour occasionally displayed by these students at home and at school was mainly due to mood swings or depression commonly experienced by individuals with intellectual disabilities and could not be construed as intentional or purposeful. Otherwise, apart from these awkward behaviour manifestations, parents claimed their children with intellectual disabilities were generally calm, self-possessed and honest. Students with intellectual disabilities would benefit from learning at school a positive interest or hobby which they should be taught to engage in during these adverse times. One of the teachers also shed light on the fact that the moral self-concept of students with intellectual disabilities depended significantly on the attitude and behaviour demonstrated by their peers towards them.

7.2.3 Personal Self-Concept

The great majority of the students with intellectual disabilities had low scores in personal self-concept. The interview responses articulated that most of the students with intellectual disabilities believed that they were helpful, kind and dependable. However, when it came to the individual's sense of personal worth and feelings of adequacy as a person, they considered themselves low in this aspect (confirmed by the questionnaire data). This is consistent with the social comparison theory (Gibbons 1986; Szivos-Bach 1993), which states that people with disabilities living in the community will make comparisons with other non-disabled groups and it is likely that their self-concept will decrease because of the negative frame of reference effects.

In this study, parents were of the opinion that their children with intellectual disabilities had the potential to display positive characteristics like reliability, responsibility and obedience; however, they were also noted to exhibit stubborn, obstinate and sensitive traits mainly because they were subjected to bullying from their non-disabled peers. This cast a negative impact on the personal self-concept of the students with intellectual disabilities which could eventually send them into long term depression. If this bullying and harassment is continued for an extended period, these students with intellectual disabilities could develop feelings of self-hatred which could signal the possibility of episodic self-destructive behaviour as suggested by Fitts and Warren (2003). This implies that the teachers and school counsellors should provide assistance and support to students with intellectual disabilities before such crisis situations arise and strive to make the classroom more inclusive for all.

One of the teachers described students with intellectual disabilities as shy, secluded and withdrawn most of the time, stating they dreaded interacting with new people lest they should be subjected to bullying and discrimination. Sometimes, students with intellectual disabilities were noted to demonstrate disorderly and troublesome behaviour which was often not intentional, but rather impulsive and abrupt, due to their intellectual discrepancy. Most teachers and parents considered that students with intellectual disabilities did not possess the capability and proficiency to solve their own problems independently, thus making them highly dependent and reliant on significant others. Often due to students' cognitive deficits, they lacked judicious and effective strategies to combat their problems in life. In spite of teachers making a conscious effort to train students on this aspect, it is still an area of serious concern.

7.2.4 Family Self-Concept

The majority of the students with intellectual disabilities had low scores in family self-concept. However, slightly less than a half of the students with intellectual disabilities obtained family self-concept scores in the normal range. Abells et al. (2008) indicated that most students with intellectual disabilities preferred to participate in activities with family members rather than with their peers.

The majority of the students with intellectual disabilities in this study claimed in the interviews to share a contented and genial relationship with most members of the family and, often with another sibling with disability. Parents and teachers articulated their views on similar lines as they believed that a child with intellectual disability always got along well with another sibling with disability. However, they reported that often tension arose between a child with intellectual disability and another sibling without disabilities or a step-parent. Parents believed that it was easier to form a good relationship with a girl with intellectual disability rather than a boy because feminine traits were known to be softer and milder compared to masculine traits. Teachers found mothers to be more considerate, thoughtful and patient towards their child with intellectual disability in comparison to fathers.

These findings suggest that in order to enhance and improve the family self-concept dimension in students with intellectual disabilities, all the members of the family need to be equally educated and responsive to the conditions and needs of the child. Parents need to devote more time to their children with intellectual disabilities and talk frankly and candidly to other family members as well, educating them about their children's disability to facilitate better co-existence and all round development of their children.

7.2.5 Social Self-Concept

The majority of the students with intellectual disabilities had low scores in social self-concept. Stanovich et al. (1998) reported similar findings to this study; they found that students who had exceptional needs scored very low on measures such as social acceptance. However, Stanovich et al. (1998) included in their research students with learning disabilities and behaviour problems, not only students with intellectual disabilities as in this present study. Therefore it was not possible to isolate or segregate the results exclusively obtained by students with diagnosed intellectual disabilities. Zic and Igric (2001) also found that students with intellectual disabilities were more often rejected by their peers. Research conducted by Abells et al. (2008) revealed that adolescents with intellectual disabilities could not interact well with their peers; the reasons mainly being their disability and lack of available supports.

In the present study, the interview responses revealed that students with intellectual disabilities portrayed themselves to be standoffish, restrained and reserved, primarily because they lacked the skills to initiate and sustain conversations. These students lacked the confidence and essential communication cues which could help them to strike up or carry on a conversation with peers. These interview findings would suggest that with more training in speaking and communication skills, students with intellectual disabilities could improve in the social self-concept dimension. Teachers and special educators need to instil a greater amount of confidence and positive communication abilities by involving these students in more and more group activities with non-disabled peers in their mainstream classes.

Parents in this research, held views similar to their children that students with intellectual disabilities lacked the competence and capability to interact with their non-disabled peers and most often were the focus of contempt and disdain in the classrooms. Teachers, however, observed an interesting trend among students with intellectual disabilities. Although, students with intellectual disabilities were noted to have fewer friends in the classrooms they appeared to compensate for this loss by establishing a good social network online. They reported students with intellectual disabilities had a close circle of friends on face book and twitter rather than in schools. Students with intellectual disabilities were also found to share a strong bond in a special setting with other students with disabilities rather than with students without disabilities. This study clearly shows that these students experienced social ineptness and discomfort in some selective contexts like the mainstream classrooms. This is indicative of the fact that true inclusion was not meted out in the mainstream classes and students with intellectual disabilities were being left out from some non-disabled mainstream peer activities. These forms of estrangement, alienation and drifting apart from their non-disabled peers in the classrooms helped to explain the low scores obtained by students with intellectual disabilities in the social self-concept dimension.

7.2.6 Academic Self-Concept

The majority of the students with intellectual disabilities had low scores in academic self-concept. In line with Fitts and Warren (2003) it can be interpreted that these students had cognitive impairments that interfered with their ability to perform in school or college settings. Results similar in nature were obtained by Crabtree (2003) and Marsh et al. (2006). Crabtree (2003) found that adolescents with mild intellectual disabilities in regular schools had considerably lower academic self-concepts. Marsh et al. (2006) however, established that those preadolescents with mild intellectual disabilities who were placed in segregated classes also had lower academic self-concepts. Since this study included students with intellectual disabilities from both mainstream and specialist settings, it is worth noting that low academic self-concept scores obtained by students with intellectual disabilities were evident in both settings. The findings are in agreement with the 'big fish little pond' theory (discussed in Chap. 3) which states that students with mild disabilities often compare themselves with peers without disabilities who perform better academically and this in turn adversely affects the self-evaluations of students with mild disabilities resulting in their low academic self-concepts (Marsh 1984). Donohue (2008) and Wiest et al. (1998) found that children with cognitive deficits who have low academic scores compensated for their loss in other non-academic arenas such as in physical abilities and socializing with peers. However, the results of the present study are not in line with Donohue (2008) and Wiest et al. (1998) findings. Students with intellectual disabilities in this study were found to obtain low scores not only in the academic self-concept but also in other non-academic dimensions of self-concept, thus casting a negative impact on the total self-concept of these students. Nevertheless it needs to be pointed out that slightly over than a quarter of the students with intellectual disabilities obtained academic self-concept scores in the normal range.

Interview responses from the students with intellectual disabilities indicated that these students possessed the ardour and impetus to learn new things and made an attempt to devise their own techniques to achieve it. This represents a positive dimension in the results. Teachers established that it often took students with intellectual disabilities longer and they required greater effort on their part to acquire new learning as compared to their non-disabled peers. This can be accredited primarily due to their cognitive deficits. Parents too found their children with intellectual disabilities to be slow and time-taking learners. One of them believed that her child construed failure too often and too early which discouraged her to spontaneously engage in any new learning. According to teachers, students with intellectual disabilities should be provided with more hands on activities and one-on-one interactions for a firmer understanding of a topic. These comments would suggest that teachers needed to provide students with intellectual disabilities with better strategies and resources to make new learning easier, exciting and spontaneous for them. These students are likely to learn well when tasks are presented to them in gradual steps and modelling may also be effective. However, as teachers usually had heavy workloads and large classes to cater for, individualized instruction and attention could not be delivered by teachers without additional resources. The lack of such support often accounted for the low academic scores obtained by students with intellectual disabilities.

7.2.7 Total Self-Concept

The great majority of the students with intellectual disabilities had low scores in total self-concept on the basis of the scoring interpretations provided in the Tennessee Self-Concept Manual. The findings showed that these students were less likely to hold a constructive image of themselves. It can be interpreted according to the work of Fitts and Warren (2003) that such individuals often felt nervous, dejected and fretful about their situation. Students with intellectual disabilities perceived themselves to be different from their non-disabled peers and most often felt stigmatized, which cast a negative influence on their overall self-concept (Abraham et al. 2002; Dagnan and Waring 2004; Gibbons 1986; Paterson et al. 2012; Szivos-Bach 1993). Participants with intellectual disabilities frequently encountered certain negative experiences (e.g. perceived intellectual inadequacy, a disproportionately high incidence of academic and social failure, social stigmatization and discrimination) and they were generally viewed as being at risk for low self-concepts (Elbaum and Sharon 2001). Similar findings were obtained by Silon and Harter (1985) and Cunningham and Glenn (2004) who indicated that students with intellectual disabilities were generally more susceptible and vulnerable towards developing a negative self-concept due to their impaired cognitive ability. Dixon et al. (2006) found that participants with mild intellectual disabilities (even after being exposed to good facilities) had low to average self-esteem compared to the normative groups on this measure. Recent research by Garaigordobil and Pérez (2007) also revealed that students with intellectual disabilities scored significantly lower in both self-concept and self-esteem.

In contradiction to the group of researchers stated above, Li et al. (2006) found that the respondents with intellectual disabilities used in their studies had surprisingly higher total self-concepts than those of a group of respondents without disabilities. However, the possible explanation for this was that the participants used the in-group social comparison to maintain positive perceptions and since most of the participants were in segregated vocational settings they easily adopted the in-group social comparison strategy. Huck et al. (2010) also found that children with intellectual disabilities integrated in mainstream classes in Sydney were able to maintain positive self-concepts. However, it should be noted that not all children were fully integrated into mainstream classes when the data was collected and therefore, the chances that these children perceived themselves to be different from their peers was limited. Duvdevany (2002) on the other hand, found the overall self-concept of individuals with intellectual disabilities who participated in integrated activities to be higher than of those who participated in segregated programmes. Similarly, Begley (1999) also found that students with Down syndrome placed in mainstream classes generally had more positive self-concepts than students in schools for children with moderate disabilities. This is indicative of the fact that students with intellectual disabilities placed in mainstream classes were able to hold positive self-concepts in some contexts, demonstrating a huge prospective for this group of students.

In the present study, there were some students with intellectual disabilities (less than a quarter) who obtained total self-concept scores in the normal range. According to the social comparison theory, when the self-concept is in jeopardy, there are three possibilities: people may minimize or limit comparisons (Brickman and Bulman 1977), avoid upward comparisons (Steil and Hay 1997) or try to self-enhance by engaging in downward comparisons (Crocker et al. 1987). It can be inferred that in this study, those students with intellectual disabilities who obtained normal self-concepts engaged in some of these three possibilities, to maintain their average self-view.

References

Abells, D., Burbidge, J., & Minnes, P. (2008). Involvement of adolescents with intellectual disabilities in social and recreational activities. *Journal on Developmental Disabilities, 14*(2), 88–94.

Abraham, C., Gregory, N., Wolf, L., & Pemberton, R. (2002). Self-esteem, stigma and community participation amongst people with learning difficulties living in the community. *Journal of Community and Applied Social Psychology, 12*(6), 430–443. doi:10.1002/casp.695.

Begley, A. (1999). The self-perceptions of pupils with Down syndrome in relation to their academic competence, physical competence and social acceptance. *International Journal of Disability, Development and Education, 46*(4), 515–529. doi:10.1080/103491299100489.

Brickman, P., & Bulman, R. J. (1977). Pleasure and pain in social comparison. In J. M. Suls & R. L. Miller (Eds.), *Social comparison processes: Theoretical and empirical perspectives* (pp. 149–186). Washington: Hemisphere.

Crabtree, J. W. (2003). Maintaining positive self-concept: Social comparisons in secondary school student with mild learning disabilities attending mainstream and special schools. In H. W. Marsh, R. G. Craven, & D. McInerney (Eds.), *International advances in self research* (Vol. 1, pp. 261–290). Greenwich: Information Age Publishing Inc.

Crocker, J., Thompson, L. L., McGraw, K. M., & Ingerman, C. (1987). Downward comparison, prejudice, and evaluations of others: Effects of self-esteem and threat. *Journal of Personality and Social Psychology, 52*(5), 907–916. doi:10.1037/0022-3514.52.5.907.

Cunningham, C., & Glenn, S. (2004). Self-awareness in young adults with Down Syndrome: Awareness of Down syndrome and disability. *International Journal of Disability, Development and Education, 51*(4), 335–361. doi:10.1080/1034912042000295017.

Dagnan, D., & Waring, M. (2004). Linking stigma to psychological distress: Testing a social–cognitive model of the experience of people with intellectual disabilities. *Clinical Psychology and Psychotherapy, 11*(4), 247–254. doi:10.1002/cpp.413.

Dixon, R. M., Craven, R., & Martin, A. (2006). *The measurement of multidimensional self-concept in adults with mild intellectual disability.* Paper presented at the Self-concept, motivation, social and personal identity for the 21st Century: Proceedings of the 4th International Biennial SELF Research Conference. Ann Arbor: University of Michigan.

Donohue, D. K. (2008). *Self-concept in children with intellectual disabilities.* Master of Arts (Psychology Theses. Paper 46), Georgia State University, Atlanta. Retrieved from http://digitalarchive.gsu.edu.proxy.library.adelaide.edu.au/psych_theses/46.

Duvdevany, I. (2002). Self-concept and adaptive behaviour of people with intellectual disability in integrated and segregated recreation activities. *Journal of Intellectual Disability Research, 46*(5), 419–429. doi:10.1046/j.1365-2788.2002.00415.x.

Elbaum, B., & Sharon, V. (2001). School-based interventions to enhance the self-concept of students with learning disabilities: A meta-analysis. *The Elementary School Journal, 101*(3), 303–329. doi:10.2307/1002249.

Fitts, W. H., & Warren, W. L. (2003). *Tennessee self-concept scale manual* (2nd ed.). Los Angeles: Western Psychological Services.

Garaigordobil, M., & Perez, J. I. (2007). Self-concept, self-esteem and psychopathological symptoms in persons with intellectual disability. *Spanish Journal of Psychology, 10*(1), 141–150.

Gibbons, F. X. (1986). Social comparison and depression: Company's effect on misery. *Journal of Personality and Social Psychology, 51*(1), 140–148. doi:10.1037/0022-3514.51.1.140.

Huck, S., Kemp, C., & Carter, M. (2010). Self-concept of children with intellectual disability in mainstream settings. *Journal of Intellectual and Developmental Disability, 35*(3), 141–154. doi:10.3109/13668250.2010.489226.

Li, E. P.-Y., Tam, A. S.-F., & Man, D. W.-K. (2006). Exploring the self-concepts of persons with intellectual disabilities. *Journal of Intellectual Disabilities, 10*(1), 19–34. doi:10.1177/1744629506062270.

Marsh, H. W. (1984). Self-concept: The application of a frame of reference model to explain paradoxical results. *Australian Journal of Education, 28*(2), 165–181.

Marsh, H. W., Tracey, D. K., & Craven, R. G. (2006). Multidimensional self-concept structure for preadolescents with mild intellectual disabilities A hybrid multigroup–MIMC approach to factorial invariance and latent mean differences. *Educational and Psychological Measurement, 66*(5), 795–818. doi:10.1177/0013164405285910.

Paterson, L., McKenzie, K., & Lindsay, B. (2012). Stigma, social comparison and self-esteem in adults with an intellectual disability. *Journal of Applied Research in Intellectual Disabilities, 25*(2), 166–176. doi:10.1111/j.1468-3148.2011.00651.x.

Silon, E. L., & Harter, S. (1985). Assessment of perceived competence, motivational orientation, and anxiety in segregated and mainstreamed educable mentally retarded children. *Journal of Educational Psychology, 77*(2), 217–230. doi:10.1037/0022-0663.77.2.217.

Stanovich, P. J., Jordan, A., & Perot, J. (1998). Relative differences in academic self-concept and peer acceptance among students in inclusive. *Remedial and Special Education, 19*(2), 120–126. doi:10.1177/074193259801900206.

Steil, J. M., & Hay, J. L. (1997). Social comparison in the workplace: A study of 60 dual-career couples. *Personality and Social Psychology Bulletin, 23*(4), 427–438. doi:10.1177/0146167297234008.

Szivos-Bach, S. E. (1993). Social comparisons, stigma and mainstreaming: The self esteem of young adults with a mild mental handicap. *Mental Handicap Research, 6*(3), 217–236. doi:10.1111/j.1468-3148.1993.tb00054.x.

Wiest, D. J., Wong, E. H., & Kreil, D. A. (1998). Predictors of global self-worth and academic performance among regular education, learning disabled, and continuation high school students. *Adolescence, 33*(131), 601–618.

Zic, A., & Igrić, L. (2001). Self-assessment of relationships with peers in children with intellectual disability. *Journal of Intellectual Disability Research, 45*(3), 202–211. doi:10.1046/j.1365-2788.2001.00311.x.

Chapter 8
Conclusion

Abstract This chapter presents the structure of the entire study, together with the research questions and answers provided by this research are drawn together towards the final conclusions. Implications for educational policy and practice and future research are also discussed. The factors leading to poor self-concepts in students with intellectual disabilities are once again recognised, summarised and stated. This chapter further outlines the implications in the classroom for teachers, special educators, teaching assistants and a range of professionals in the education sector catering to the needs of students with intellectual disabilities. Future intensive investigation is required to ensure that educational and support services adequately meet the needs of these students and provide them with the knowledge and skills to effectively interact in society and achieve the highest quality of life possible.

Keywords Self-concept · Students with intellectual disabilities · Social skills training · Policy and practice · Dimensions of self-concept

8.1 Structure of the Study

The purpose of this chapter is to restate the structural and informational content of this study together with the outcomes, its implications for educational policy and practice and recommendations for future initiatives. This research has been a small scale qualitative study which has provided a limited basis for generalizing to any wider population beyond the participants themselves. Nevertheless, the richness of its data has provided deeper understandings and insights into the self-concepts for students with intellectual disabilities.

This study determined the self-concept of these students (females and males) placed in specialist and mainstream settings in South Australia. The self-concept scores were investigated across the dimensions namely Physical, Moral, Personal, Family, Social, Academic Self-Concepts and Total Self-Concept. The study provided insights into what students with intellectual disabilities were able to achieve

P. Datta, *Students with Intellectual Disabilities*, SpringerBriefs in Education,
DOI: 10.1007/978-981-287-017-9_8, © The Author(s) 2014

in the different dimensions of self-concept and identified the reasons for their high or low self-concepts. The central research questions that guided this study were:

- What are the scores of self-concept and its dimensions for the female and male students with intellectual disabilities in South Australia?
- What are students with intellectual disabilities able to achieve in the different dimensions of self-concept and why?

In view of the recognition, acceptance and inclusion of the different and multiple dimensions of self-concept, the present research was guided by the Shavelson et al. (1976) and Marsh and Shavelson (1985) models of self-concept and other recent research studies (Duvdevany 2002; Tracey and Marsh 2002). This project was conducted in two Stages namely Stage 1 and Stage 2. In Stage 1, the Tennessee Self-Concept questionnaire was administered to students (females and males) with intellectual disabilities to determine their self-concept scores on the different dimensions. In Stage 2, interviews with specific students with intellectual disabilities, their parents and teachers were conducted to understand what students with intellectual disabilities were able to accomplish in the different dimensions of self-concept and why self-concepts were low or high in these students under investigation.

8.2 Findings

In summarizing and discussing the findings of this study, answers are provided to the two research questions advanced in Chap. 1.

8.2.1 Research Question 1

What are the scores of self-concept and its dimensions for the female and male students with intellectual disabilities in South Australia?

The exact self-concept T-scores are reported in detail in Chap. 5, but they are restated here in broader terms to provide a more holistic picture across the dimensions of self-concept for females and males with intellectual disabilities.

The self-concept scores (high/average/low) across the Physical, Moral, Personal, Family, Social, Academic and Total self-concepts for the female and male students with intellectual disabilities are represented in Table 8.1.

Table 8.1 indicates the overall pattern of responses across the different dimensions of self-concept for students with intellectual disabilities. There were no scores in the high range across the different dimensions of self-concept. In case of the male students, the highest frequency of average scores was in the family self-concept. For male students, the self-concept dimensions with the highest

Table 8.1 Frequency of T-scores across self-concept dimensions for female and male students with intellectual disabilities (N = 20)

Dimensions of self-concept	Female (N = 10)			Male (N = 10)			Total (N = 20)		
	High	Average (%)	Low (%)	High	Average (%)	Low (%)	High	Average (%)	Low (%)
Physical	–	20	80	–	–	100		10	90
Moral	–	40	60	–	20	80	–	30	70
Personal	–	20	80	–	10	90	–	15	85
Family	–	50	50	–	30	70	–	40	60
Social	–	50	50	–	10	90	–	30	70
Academic	–	50	50	–	20	80	–	35	65
Total[a]	–	30	70	–	–	100	–	15	85

[a] Total self-concept for each student is calculated as the sum of the dimensions 'raw to T' scores and not the arithmetical average of the individual dimensions

frequency of low scores were physical followed equally by personal and social. In case of the female students, the highest average scores were in the family, social and academic self-concept dimensions (an equal number in the three dimensions respectively). For female students, the highest numbers of low scores were in the physical and personal self-concept dimensions.

Overall (male and female students combined) the two dimensions of self-concept with highest average frequency was family followed by academic and the two dimensions of self-concept with highest low frequency was physical followed by personal.

8.2.2 Research Question 2

What are students with intellectual disabilities able to achieve in the different dimensions of self-concept and why?

In exploring this research question, the interviewees indicated that students with intellectual disabilities could not achieve well in the different dimensions of self-concept and went on to explain in detail the reasons behind this. A number of key reasons were identified for low self-concepts among students with intellectual disabilities. One related to the degree and severity of impairment suffered (the greater the impairment the lower the self-concept). Another involved personal factors such as lack of independence, cognitive deficits, depression and mood swings. Indifferent or negative behaviour demonstrated by non-disabled mainstream peers, such as lack of support or even outright bullying represents another set of reasons for low self-concept. School factors such as inexperienced and unskilled teachers, lack of confidence and exclusion from mainstream classes, as well as family factors such as inadequate support at home and step-parent households, also contributed to low self-concept. As a result of such influences these students experienced failure too often and too early and they took more time and required extra effort to learn and grasp new concepts.

Thus, the findings discussed above leads to two strong and clear conclusions. First, consistently low scores were obtained by the majority of students with intellectual disabilities in the different dimensions of self-concept. Second, the teachers' interview responses have most often been in contrast to the responses provided by students with intellectual disabilities and their parents across all the themes used for the interview analysis. The following sections present implications for educational policy, practice and future research and concluding comments.

8.3 Implications for Policy and Practice

The findings of this study have the potential to influence teaching practices and drive future investigations relating to students with intellectual disabilities.

The findings revealed that the majority of the students with intellectual disabilities had low total self-concepts. For students with low self-concepts, interventions that include parents and teachers can be especially effective (Fitts and Warren 2003). The findings of this study indicate that parent involvement remains useful and a teacher who establishes more personal contact may also prove effective.

Students with intellectual disabilities obtained the highest frequency of average (normal) scores (refer Table 8.1) in the family and academic self-concept dimensions. This indicates the positive influence of the two groups—family and school on these students. Students with intellectual disabilities obtained the highest frequency of low scores (refer Table 8.1) in the personal and physical self-concept dimensions. This is indicative of the fact that these students need adequate support and assistance to increase their low sense of worth which is often related primarily to a weak sense of identity. These students also need a more directed, planned and structured routine of activities in relation to maintaining their physical lives which needs to be imbibed from inception years in school. For those students with intellectual disabilities with disturbed physical self-concepts, self-acceptance can be a particularly important part of positive change. The findings from this study suggest that physical exercises, relaxation, breathing, or stretching movements are often beneficial to these students.

Findings from the research indicate that students with intellectual disabilities require a structured social skills program to assist them to develop a flexible repertoire of appropriate role behaviours, and learn the procedure for joining groups, interacting in groups, and conforming to group rules. They also need to understand what is important and meaningful to the group, and learn their rules for socializing and making friends. Students with intellectual disabilities have to deal with the fact that they are perceived as different from their peers. Social skills training to gain skill in making eye contact, body posture, interpret body language, appropriate ways to initiate interactions, engaging in small talk, assertive training to gain expertise in articulating desires and coping with the consequences, appropriate self-disclosure and appropriate boundary setting all may provide excellent ways for these students to begin to meet goals related to improving relationships and social interactions. Schools need to develop a whole school approach to social skills training and social awareness for these students.

The rich data set generated from this project will benefit teachers, special educators, policy makers and a range of professionals in the education and special education sector to raise awareness of the many areas these students experience problems in and which could serve as a potential catalyst for such students. Professional development for teachers which focuses on deepening their understanding about the condition of any students' disability, and increased awareness of the nature of intellectual disability and the educational implications of this disability must be a priority for teachers, families, students with intellectual disabilities, as well as other non-disabled peers and society in general.

8.4 Implications for Future Research

The present research study investigated the self-concept among students with intellectual disabilities in South Australia. However, students with other kinds of disabilities (e.g. students with hearing impairments, vision impairments, learning disabilities, physical impairments, autism and attention deficit hyperactive disorder) commonly found in the classrooms in Australia were not included in the research. Similar facets should be studied for students with other disabilities as well. Moreover, this research was conducted in South Australia; there is a need to replicate this investigation in the other states of Australia in order to verify the validity of these findings.

References

Duvdevany, I. (2002). Self-concept and adaptive behaviour of people with intellectual disability in integrated and segregated recreation activities. *Journal of Intellectual Disability Research, 46*(5), 419–429. doi:10.1046/j.1365-2788.2002.00415.x.

Fitts, W. H., & Warren, W. L. (2003). *Tennessee self-concept scale manual* (2nd ed.). Los Angeles, CA: Western Psychological Services.

Marsh, H. W., & Shavelson, R. (1985). Self-concept: Its multifaceted, hierarchical structure. *Educational Psychologist, 20*(3), 107–123. doi:10.1207/s15326985ep2003_1.

Shavelson, R. J., Hubner, J. J., & Stanton, G. C. (1976). Self-concept: Validation of construct interpretations. *Review of Educational Research, 46*(3), 407–441.

Tracey, D. K., & Marsh, H. W. (2002). Self-concepts of preadolescents with mild intellectual disability: Multidimensionality, measurement, and support for the big fish little pond effect. *Self-Concept Research: Driving International Research Agendas, 35*, 419–427.

Appendix A

Scoring Worksheet

See Fig. A.1.

P. Datta, *Students with Intellectual Disabilities*, SpringerBriefs in Education,
DOI: 10.1007/978-981-287-017-9, © The Author(s) 2014

Adult Form **TSCS:2**

Scoring Instructions

Published by
wps WESTERN PSYCHOLOGICAL SERVICES
Publishers and Distributors

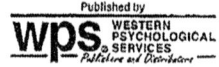

Client's Name: __SAMPLE__

FULL FORM — Note: If any item response is missing or double-marked, circle the median response value (printed in bold type) for that item on the Scoring Worksheet.

Determine INC raw score
To determine the Inconsistent Responding (INC) raw score, refer to the Scoring Worksheet. Enter the response values for each item pair in the spaces provided here to the right. Then enter the absolute value of the difference in response values (i.e., the simple size of the difference, regardless of which response value is larger) in the "Difference" spaces provided. The INC raw score is the sum of these differences. Enter that number in the space provided for the INC raw score on the side of the Profile Sheet that corresponds to the client's age.

Calculate FG raw score
To calculate the Faking Good (FG) raw score, refer to the Scoring Worksheet. For each item specified below, copy the response value into the space provided. Then calculate as directed. Transfer the result to the space provided for the FG raw score on the Profile Sheet.

Inconsistent Responding (INC) Score

				Difference
Item 1	**4**	and Item 69	**4**	→ **0** (1)
Item 3	**5**	and Item 65	**4**	→ **1**
Item 6	**4**	and Item 44	**4**	→ **0**
Item 7	**5**	and Item 20	**4**	→ **1**
Item 9	**3**	and Item 43	**5**	→ **2**
Item 10	**3**	and Item 77	**3**	→ **0**
Item 13	**5**	and Item 15	**5**	→ **0**
Item 21	**5**	and Item 58	**4**	→ **1**
Item 29	**5**	and Item 30	**5**	→ **0**

INC Raw Score: **5**

(3) **Faking Good (FG) Score**

$$(\underset{\text{Item 1}}{4} + \underset{\text{Item 3}}{5} + \underset{\text{Item 21}}{5} + \underset{\text{Item 22}}{4} + \underset{\text{Item 64}}{4}) - (\underset{\text{Item 28}}{3} + \underset{\text{Item 41}}{4}) = \boxed{15} \text{ FG Raw Score}$$

Determine RD raw score
To obtain the Response Distribution (RD) raw score, count the number of 1s and 5s circled on the Scoring Worksheet. Enter this number in the space provided for the RD raw score on the Profile Sheet.

Calculate remaining raw scores
To calculate the remaining raw scores, refer to the Scoring Worksheet. Copy each item's response value into the boxes in the same row. Add up the numbers in each column and record the subtotals in the spaces provided at the bottom of each page. Transfer the column subtotals from the first page of the Worksheet to the designated spaces at the bottom of the second page. Sum the two subtotals for each column to obtain the raw score for that scale. Transfer the raw scores to the spaces provided at the bottom of the Profile Sheet. Use the spaces provided at the bottom of the second page of the Worksheet to calculate the Total (TOT) raw score and the Net Conflict (CON) raw score. The TOT raw score is the sum of the Physical, Moral, Personal, Family, Social, and Academic/Work raw scores. To calculate the CON raw score, multiply the Negative (NEG) raw score by 2, and subtract it from the TOT raw score.

Plot profile to obtain *T*-scores and percentiles
Plot each scale's raw score on the Profile Sheet by placing a mark over its value in the appropriate column. The corresponding *T*-score and percentile rank can be found along the left and right margins of the profile, in the same row where the raw score appears. Enter the *T*-scores in the designated spaces along the lower margin of the Profile Sheet.

SHORT FORM — Note: If any item response is missing or double-marked, circle the median response value (printed in bold type) for that item on the Scoring Worksheet.

Calculate raw score
Note that only a Short Form total score can be calculated. On the Scoring Worksheet, add together the response values for Items 1–20 and circle the resulting total on the "Raw Scores" line of the following graph.

Obtain *T*-score
To determine the Short Form *T*-score, refer to the graph shown below. In the row of *T*-scores for this client's age group, circle the *T*-score that corresponds to the Short Form raw score you have circled. (This graph is an abbreviated version of Appendix A in the TSCS:2 Manual, which also contains Short Form percentile scores.)

T-scores for Ages 13–18:	<20	20	24	26	28	29	31	33	35	37	39	40	42	44	46	47	49	51	53	55	57	58	60	62	65	68	69	71	76	>80
Raw Scores:	20–43	44	46	48	50	52	54	56	58	60	62	64	66	68	70	72	74	76	78	80	82	84	86	88	90	92	94	96	98	100
T-scores for Ages 21+:	<20	22	23	24	27	28	29	30	31	33	35	37	39	41	42	44	46	49	51	53	55	57	59	61	64	66	69	73	79	

12031 Wilshire Boulevard • Los Angeles, California 90025-1251

W-320A

Fig. A.1 Completed TSCS: 2 adult autoscore™ form

TSCS:2 Scoring Worksheet

(6)

SC	NEG	IDN	SAT	BHV	PHY	MOR	PER	FAM	SOC	ACA	Item	Response Values (circled)
		4			4						1.	4
		5				5					2.	5
		5						5			3.	5
	4		4			4					4.	4
	2			2					2		5.	2
	4									4	6.	4
		5							5		7.	5
			4			4					8.	4
	3									3	9.	3
	3			3				3			10.	3
			4				4				11.	4
										3	12.	3
			5					5			13.	5
	3		3				3				14.	3
			5					5			15.	5
	5		5				1.5				16.	5
	3		3		3						17.	3
										3	18.	3
			4				4				19.	4
				14					4		20.	4
		5			5						21.	5
	4	4			4						22.	4
		4				4					23.	4
	3			3			3				24.	3
		4					4				25.	4
	5	5					5				26.	5
		5						5			27.	5
3											28.	3
	5	5			5						29.	5
	5	5			1.5						30.	5
	4	4				4					31.	4
										4	32.	4
	5	5					5				33.	5
	5	5					1.5				34.	5
	5	5						5			35.	5
	5	5						5			36.	5
	3									3	37.	3
	5	5							5		38.	5
	4	4							4		39.	4
3											40.	3
4											41.	4
10	85	89	37	12	26	21	38	33	20	20	Raw score subtotals from this page	
SC	NEG	IDN	SAT	BHV	PHY	MOR	PER	FAM	SOC	ACA		

(7)

Fig. A.1 (Continued)

Client's Name: **SAMPLE**

SC	NEG	IDN	SAT	BHV	PHY	MOR	PER	FAM	SOC	ACA	Response Values
			5		5						42. ⑤ 4 3 2 1
	5									5	43. 1 2 3 4 ⑤
										4	44. 5 ④ 3 2 1
			4						4		45. 5 ④ 3 2 1
	3			3		3					46. 1 2 ③ 4 5
4											47. 5 ④ 3 2 1
	2		2		2						48. 1 ② 3 4 5
	4		4			4					49. 1 2 3 ④ 5
	5									5	50. 1 2 3 4 ⑤
			5				5				51. ⑤ 4 3 2 1
	4		4				4				52. 1 2 3 ④ 5
	2		2				2				53. 1 ② 3 4 5
			4						4		54. 5 ④ 3 2 1
	2		2						2		55. 1 ② 3 4 5
2											56. 5 4 3 ② 1
3											57. 5 4 ③ 2 1
				4	4						58. 5 ④ 3 2 1
				5	5						59. ⑤ 4 3 2 1
				4		4					60. 5 ④ 3 2 1
	4			4		4					61. 1 2 3 ④ 5
				4			4				62. 5 ④ 3 2 1
										4	63. 5 ④ 3 2 1
				4	4						64. 5 ④ 3 2 1
				4				4			65. 5 ④ 3 2 1
				4					4		66. 5 ④ 3 2 1
5											67. ⑤ 4 3 2 1
	4			4	4						68. 1 2 3 ④ 5
			4		4						69. 5 ④ 3 2 1
	5									5	70. 1 2 3 4 ⑤
	5										71. 1 2 3 4 ⑤
				5		5					72. ⑤ 4 3 2 1
	3		3						3		73. 1 2 ③ 4 5
				3		3					74. 5 4 ③ 2 1
	5	5			1.5						75. 1 2 3 4 ⑤
			3		3						76. 5 4 ③ 2 1
	3		3				3				77. 1 2 ③ 4 5
				3					3		78. 5 4 ③ 2 1
	2		2				2				79. 1 ② 3 4 5
3											80. 5 4 ③ 2 1
										3	81. 5 4 ③ 2 1
		5				5					82. ② 4 3 2 1
17	58	10	42	61	33	28	12	18	22	26	Raw score subtotals from this page ⑦
10	85	89	37	12	26	21	38	33	20	20	Plus raw score subtotals from previous page ⑧
27	143	99	79	73	59	49	50	51	42	46	RAW SCORES ⑨
SC	NEG	IDN	SAT	BHV	PHY	MOR	PER	FAM	SOC	ACA	

$$\underline{59}_{PHY} + \underline{49}_{MOR} + \underline{50}_{PER} + \underline{51}_{FAM} + \underline{42}_{SOC} + \underline{46}_{ACA} = \boxed{297} \ ⑪$$

Total Raw Score (TOT)

$$\underline{143}_{NEG} \times 2 = \boxed{286}$$

$$\underline{297}_{TOT} - \underline{286}_{NEG \times 2} = \boxed{11} \ ⑬$$

Net Conflict Raw Score (CON)

Fig. A.1 (Continued)

Appendix B

Profile Sheet

See Fig. B.1.

P. Datta, *Students with Intellectual Disabilities*, SpringerBriefs in Education, DOI: 10.1007/978-981-287-017-9, © The Author(s) 2014

Adult Form Ages 19-90

TSCS:2 Profile Sheet
W.H. Fitts, Ph.D. and W.L. Warren, Ph.D.

Client's Name: SAMPLE

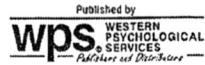

Published by
WPS WESTERN PSYCHOLOGICAL SERVICES
Publishers and Distributors

Raw Scores	5	27	15	27	297	11	59	49	50	51	42	46	99	79	73
T-Scores	50	49	57	49	50	65	59	46	51	52	39	49	59	48	44
	INC	SC	FC	RD	TOT	CON	PHY	MOR	PER	FAM	SOC	ACA	IDN	SAT	BHV

Mark scores higher than 80T and lower than 20T along the corresponding edge of the profile.

12031 Wilshire Boulevard • Los Angeles, California 90025-1251

W-320A

Fig. B.1 Completed TSCS: 2 adult autoscore™ form

CPSIA information can be obtained at www.ICGtesting.com
Printed in the USA
LVOW10s2144120614

389875LV00003B/27/P